Unless You're The Lead Dog, The Scenery Never Changes

What the Professionals are saying

Just finished my second read through. What a great job. I am proud of you and the fact that you have taken the time and energy to pass on your seasoned advice to young men and women who will be fulfilling all of the positions you have outlined, now and in the future.

This book is straight from the shoulder advice that will reap success. A 'GRAND SLAM' it rounded all the bases of advice for success. If you want to be the 'RAM ROD' of this outfit - a must read and anyone can benefit from the books solid points of experience. It is honest, straight forward and useful, and easy to read.

Brad Gates, Orange County Sheriff – (retired)

Good police officers learn from their experience on the streets. Exceptional police officers also learn from the experience of others. Hopefully, you will learn the art of becoming competent in promotional exams by the experience of others and not by your own repetitive failures.

As a former police officer, I know all too well the frustrations of failing a promotional examination. I only wish Chief Elvin Miali's book had been written during my law enforcement career as it would have saved me frustration and disappointment. I know you can learn from his many years of success as a Chief of Police and personal mentor to numerous officers.

I highly recommend you study the various techniques provided in his book, "*Unless You're The Lead Dog, The Scenery Never Changes.*" Don't be a casualty of your own

lack of understanding of the promotional system.
Keith Duckworth, Executive Vice President, Administrative Services And Human Resources Hyundai Motor America. Former Police Officer

If you aspire to successfully compete for promotion in your agency, *Unless You're The Lead Dog, The Scenery Never Changes* can help you achieve your goal. El Miali provides valuable insight into the preparation and strategy required to successfully compete in today's highly competitive environment.
Paul Sorrell, Police Chief, Fountain Valley Police Department

If you want to advance in responsibility and leadership positions, this book is for you. Chief Miali obviously decided early in his career that he wanted to see "the scenery change." He evolved a strategy for promoting. In addition to gaining knowledge about his profession, Chief Miali learned how to present himself and his information to those evaluating his competence. He learned how to make himself appear to be a better candidate than his competitors. That is, he quickly realized that it is not enough to *be* the best applicant; one must also *appear* to be the best applicant.

As his experience and information increased, he became a repository of an enormous amount of information. This book represents Chief Miali's accumulated knowledge of everything he has learned relative to promoting in a public safety agency. It is also the reader's opportunity to take advantage of Chief Miali's experience and enter the promotion process ahead of your competitors, who have not had the advantage of this preparation.

Chief Miali's knowledge of the subject is extensive, experientially obtained, well organized, and presented in a manner that is clear and easy to read. This book should be an essential part of your preparation for <u>all</u> promotional exams. − *Dr. Stuart Shaffer, Police Psychologist*

This book is a no nonsense approach to attaining your ultimate goals, from Senior Officer to Chief. I know because as a Lieutenant and Captain I worked for Chief Miali during his tenure at Fountain Valley Police Department.

Without his guidance, mentorship and encouragement I would NEVER have attained my career goals.

I must emphasize there are no free rides when you work for Chief Miali. He was open to all who asked, and all you needed to do was take the first step. Just like this book --- it is your first step."

Robert Mosley, Police Captain (retired)

... The firefighter will find, *Unless you're The Lead Dog The Scenery Never Changes,* very beneficial.

It goes beyond mere professional inquisition. It defines the mental and physical aspects necessary to succeed in the promotional process no matter what discipline you are involved with. The book is designed to assist anyone who is involved in an Oral Board or Assessment Center presentation. I would recommend this book to any firefighter that is preparing for a promotional exam.

Mark Haskell, Fire Chief, Fountain Valley Fire Department

This book is a very easy read with common sense stuff that certainly worked for me. Besides all of the studying and preparation, there are two things that seemed to help me prepare for each promotional; the meetings with Chief Miali and the "Standards for Career Development" within the department that he set forth early on. Every Chief of Police has the duty to provide that "road map" for his personnel to follow if they chose to as I did.

I honestly believe the promotional process starts the day you are hired and pin that badge on. Your peers, supervisors and citizens alike begin judging and forming opinions about you immediately...it will set you apart from the others.

Chief, you have a winner. I would suggest this book to anyone who plans on promoting sometime in their career. This is an excellent guide to follow and should be read early on in one's career, not just prior to promotion. -

Dann Bean, Police Captain (retired)

Unless You're The Lead Dog, The Scenery Never Changes

A Police Chief's Insight
On How to Properly
Prepare for Public Safety
Promotional Exams

Elvin G. Miali

Police Chief Retired

Printed in the United States of America

Written by Elvin G. Miali

ISBN 0-9769393-0-4

Visit our website:

www.leaddogpromotions.com

Dedication

This book is dedicated to my beautiful wife, Charli who gave me the idea and the encouragement to complete this book as well as my children Elvin and Carla who gave me solid input and support throughout this project. I love all of you.

Acknowledgements

I wish to thank everyone who took time from their busy schedules to proof read this book and to give their opinions on the quality of its contents.

CONTENTS

Introduction

CONTENTS

Introduction

Unless You're The Lead Dog, The Scenery Never Changes.

Choose a job you love and you will never "work" another day in your life!!!

If you look forward to challenges, enjoy the unknown, have the ability to develop others, constantly think "outside the box," and you're not afraid of taking responsibility for your actions then you will have a great time being a Supervisor!

During the promotional process, I know what administrators are looking for in their personnel, and I will share this inside information with you so you will have an edge over your competition.

I want to turn any of your negative thinking into positive thoughts, remove your doubts, and make you confident in your abilities. **Unless you're the lead dog, the scenery never changes** says it all. In this book, you will gain insight into the promotional process that can only "come from the top." My goal in developing this primer is to make you the most competitive individual as well as the best prepared candidate in the promotional process.

I have taken experiences, good and bad, that I have encountered throughout my vast 37- year career, which included situations that worked and other situations that "stank" and incorporated them into a positive experience

9

that will help you enjoy - yes I said enjoy - this great experience of your career.

Many of you may be asking yourself, "Who is this guy, and why should I take his advice?" A very valid question and I feel it is only fair that I give you my background in Law Enforcement as well as my experience with the promotional process.

I began my career as a police officer in 1967 in the city of San Gabriel, located in Los Angeles County, California. After three and - a - half years in the Patrol Division, I was assigned to the Detective Bureau where I eventually spent 12 years. Six of those years I was assigned to Robbery / Homicide. I made the rank of Detective Sergeant and a year later was promoted to Lieutenant and reassigned to the Patrol Division. After working as a Watch Commander I returned to Investigations as the Detective Bureau Commander. When I completed my stint in the Detective Bureau, I attained the rank of Captain in charge of operations. In 1986, after completing a rigorous testing process which included an Assessment Center and an Oral Board before the City Council, I was selected Chief of Police for the City of Fountain Valley in Orange County, California. I remained in this position for 17 years. According to the Orange County Police and Sheriffs Association, until my retirement from Law Enforcement in late October of 2003, I was the longest tenured Police Chief in Orange County.

During my career, I have been involved in numerous testing processes, which included Oral Board presentations and Assessment Centers. This book will provide you with an insider's perspective from both sides of the testing process.

Throughout my career in Law Enforcement, and especially during my tenure as Police Chief, I was constantly gathering information on how to properly prepare for promotional exams. These exams have not been solely for Law Enforcement as I have also sat as a rater for Battalion Chief promotional oral boards as well as being one of the primary interviewers for a Fire Chief's position. As a Department Administrator, I was involved with the reshaping of many of these promotional processes so that I could evaluate and choose the best possible candidate for the position.

Observing what takes place on both sides of the table has been extremely beneficial to me throughout my career, and I know that these experiences will assist you. As an Administrator, I have developed many promotional programs, including the selection of qualified raters, developing parameters for qualified candidates, and the gathering of information for questions to be used during the Chief's interview.

I also know how it feels *not* to reach your goals with regards to a promotion. How do I know this? During my first promotional process for a Sergeant's position, I failed my written exam. This book will go into greater detail regarding this incident and how to avoid the mistakes I made, including the time when the Police Chief passed me over for a Captain's position and chose the number two candidate, even though I scored number one, in the 90th percentile, on the eligibility list. To this day, this demonstrates that attaining the highest score *does not* guarantee you a promotion. These were major set backs for me, which could have easily sent me into a negative spiral and cost me my career. Believe me, I know how you feel. I know how much it hurts, and how difficult it can be when you are not appointed to the position you have been striving to attain. I have to tell you that these alleged calamities in my career also gave me the resolve to change a negative situation into a positive, enabling me to eventually attain my goal as Chief of Police.

My experiences set down in this book will help you develop strategies on how to handle these situations in attaining your goals.

Many employees from the public and private sectors approach me requesting information on how to properly prepare for their promotional process. I provide one-on-one counseling sessions with them and discuss various ways they can prepare themselves for their upcoming promotional exams. I constantly receive feedback that these one-on-one counseling sessions are very beneficial to the candidates, and since I *know* this information assisted them, I decided to write this book, so that you may also take advantage of my experience. Promotional exams shouldn't be the end of everything that you have accomplished throughout your career; instead, they should be an experience to open new horizons on which you can build your future.

Don't set yourself up for failure. I can't tell you how many times I've heard a candidate convince themselves, prior to stepping through the door, " I don't take written exams very well" or "Man, I really freeze during the Oral

Board presentations." These candidates are setting themselves up for failure. As Henry Ford once said, "If you believe you can or you believe you can't, you're right." This book will help you overcome these negative thoughts and provide you with an opportunity to know exactly what to expect and how to prepare for your promotional process. It will assist you in making the best presentation possible during this promotional experience.

Since you are the master of your own destiny, why not make the best of it?

Remember being promoted or making rank is the most important aspect of your career. This is the "Brass Ring" on the Merry Go Round; the "Pot of Gold" at the end of the Rainbow; the "Grand Finale" that you have been striving for all these years; the culmination for all of your hard earned work.

Now is the time to get on board and get ready for the time of your life. You will view the promotional experience with a totally different understanding. So, be excited about the upcoming promotion and look forward to a new adventure so that you can become the **"Lead Dog."**

Good luck and remember that no matter what may happen to you during this journey, always keep your outlook positive.

Now, let's begin our adventure.

Chapter 1

Is This the Right Time to Take the "Leadership Plunge"?

"It is not enough to do what is best, you must do whatever is necessary" - Winston Churchill

When you decide that the time is "right" to take the "Leadership Plunge" and test for a Supervisory position within your Department, you have several things to consider.

When you become a Supervisor, there will be numerous changes that will occur with you and your position within the Department. I usually relate this to various positions of a baseball team. For example:

As an **Officer** you are one of the players on the field involved in the day-to-day activities such as making arrests, going to court, or being involved in various assignments etc. You are the star player!

When you promote to the rank of **Sergeant,** things will start to change, for the better. You become the sideline coach of the team, still on the playing field, but not as involved as before. As a Sergeant (which I believe is one of the most important positions in the Department), you are a first line Supervisor and have direct contact with all of the troops. You monitor all of their activities, develop your personnel, and are a direct conduit from the troops to the administration. Basically, you are keeping the pulse of the organization by having first hand information as to what the troops are thinking and need as

14

well as what the Administration is thinking and what their needs are.

When you reach the rank of **Lieutenant**, this position is similar to the manager of the team. You are in the dugout, off the field for the most part, but still in charge of everything that takes place "between the lines." You are even more involved in the development of your personnel and the evaluation of their performance.

As a **Captain**, you have become the General Manager, off the field and watching the game from the GM's box. As a Division Commander, you are now responsible for your officers and Supervisors. You develop these personnel so they perform as a unit and they have the same philosophy as the Chief of Police.

When you have reached the rank of **Chief of Police**, you are the owner of the team, away from the active day to day involvement out in the field, but responsible for the sworn, and non-sworn personnel who help run the Department. Not only do you monitor **everything**, you are **responsible** for everything and the "buck stops at your desk."

Utilizing this analogy is the easiest way that I can explain some of the changes that may take place when you begin to promote through the ranks. As you can see, it is exciting to watch how in each position you can participate in the development of your personnel, your Department, and especially yourself.

Now is the time to obtain the job description for the position you are attempting to attain. Your Personnel Department should have these documents, which are very important because they will tell you exactly what your Department is looking for in the candidate testing for this position. Review these job descriptions and verify that you have met all of the qualifications necessary for the position. Keep them handy because we will refer to them later on in the book.

Something else to consider is that each Agency has its own personality or "culture." This is determined by many variables such as the citizens of your community, the City Council, the City Manager, and the Chief of Police. "Culture" can best be defined as, "the belief and values of a group." This group has shared attitudes and the same philosophy. Therefore, no two Agencies are alike. For example, we all are involved in Law Enforcement but the way we enforce these laws, and how we provide customer service to our citizens differs from Agency to Agency. The "culture" of the organization along with the philosophy of the Chief of Police dictates the policy and procedures on how the Officers and Supervisors are expected to act in the field.

Is your agency pro-active or reactive? Does your Department have a "get in your face" attitude with all contacts or does it endorse a "Community Oriented Policing" philosophy and only "gets in your face" when the situation requires it? You probably already know the expectations of your agency by observing the actions of your immediate Supervisors and how the Chief of Police runs his or her Department. If you are uncomfortable with these actions and do not feel that you can actively participate as a Supervisor in this environment, then don't take the exam. If you truly want to be a Supervisor, then it is probably the right time to look for another Agency whose "culture" and philosophy you can support. This will also assist you in achieving your goals. Once you know the "culture" of your organization and make the decision to support it, you are ready to continue to the next phase.

This phase requires you to take a lot of time and ask yourself a very important question regarding this promotional process. You must be very honest and ask yourself, "Do I really want the position and why?" Think it over; don't just say, "Because I know I can do it!" After giving this question some serious thought and determining that you *do* want the position, read on.

The next two sections cover areas that relate to both the **Positives** and what I call **Concerns** for becoming a Supervisor. When you have finished reading these sections, I have another self - examination for you to complete in the **Honest Reflection** section.

Chapter 2

So What Are Some of the Positives for Becoming a Supervisor?

I believe one of the best reasons for becoming a Supervisor is that you will be a manager in your agency and be a vital player in the development of your subordinates and the Department; this should be a prime motivational factor for you. Naturally, there is the monetary incentive that comes with every promotion, which is very important when planning for your future.

As a Supervisor, you demonstrate *your* leadership abilities. How great is that? Remember when you used to sit around with your fellow officers and tell them how you could handle a situation so much better than your current Supervisor? This is nothing new; we all did it. This kind of banter is a good thing to participate in as long as you maintain proper respect and continue to follow the orders of your Supervisor. This exchange of ideas actually helps to develop your own leadership abilities because you will start to think like a Supervisor, which is very important. In fact, if you think about it, it is similar to voting in an election. There is a saying that "if you didn't vote in the election, don't complain about who's in office." It's the same about becoming a Supervisor. If you feel you would be a good Supervisor and could assist in improving your Department and the service that is provided to your citizens, then being promoted is your "vote" or opportunity to provide input on changes you feel are necessary. Or if your Department is running smoothly, then you can maintain the status quo.

As a Supervisor you will be able to develop information on the best ways to improve procedures and policies that are for the good of the Department. You see, as a Supervisor your voice can be heard and you can influence not only your superiors, but also your troops.

Becoming a Supervisor is a great thing, something you've worked for during your entire career. It is more than just giving orders or assigning Officers to a beat every day.

- You are in charge of every situation that occurs out in the field.

- You will review all of the actions of your Officers and determine what training may be useful in their development.

- You can create scenarios or situations for training purposes.

You will face new challenges such as becoming a mentor, a confidant, a cheerleader, a disciplinarian, and you will be able to help other personnel develop their breadth of knowledge in their chosen profession. With your assistance, some day they can advance in their career.

You will become a role model to many. Some Officers may not tell you to your face, but you can be sure that if you have been doing your job correctly, you will make an impact. Others will tell you how much you have meant to their career and how they have patterned their own career after yours.

You will be proud that you, as a Supervisor, were able to make such a difference. This is one of the highest tributes that anyone can bestow on you. Believe me, your world will change because of it!

As a Police Chief, I considered all of my Supervisors as management, and it didn't matter if they were first-line Supervisor Sergeants or Captains. Now I want you to understand I am not speaking for every Police Chief because we all have our own way of handling various Supervisory positions, but here is my thinking on the situation. Let's say you are a Sergeant, working a graveyard shift. There's no Lieutenant on duty and the Police Chief is home sleeping, knowing that *his* City is being protected by the finest Supervisor he has on his shift that night--you. It doesn't matter that you are the only Supervisor on duty that night-- you are the best one he has out there. Think about it. Who is in charge? YOU. If a major situation develops, who will handle it? YOU. If there are notifications to be made, who is going to make the decision to make those notifications? YOU. So, to my way of thinking, it stands to reason that you are the Supervisor in charge, that is the Chief of Police, and that means you are management not just for this one night but throughout your Supervisory career. (Remember, we are talking about leadership positions not M.O.U. (Memorandum of Understanding) issues or Personnel job descriptions). That is what makes the position of Supervisor so great because you are the main person in charge, and you can develop others who in turn will help develop the future of your Department.

Chapter 3

Let's Discuss a Few Areas of Concern When You Become a Supervisor

If, after you have examined the situation, and determined that money is the *only* reason for wanting to promote, then please don't do it. At the very least, public service is always our goal. That is why most of us entered public safety as a career. You will not be a good Supervisor nor will you be of any benefit to your subordinates or the Department. Being a Supervisor takes someone who wants to be involved with his subordinates and the City in which he works and not just pick up a paycheck. So, if money is your only motivation don't waste your time nor the City's time and money.

This will be a new position, one that you are not totally familiar with, and it will take time for you to learn what is expected of you. You should also understand that there will be time constraints and as a Supervisor, you will be expected to work various shifts and be available when required by the Department. You will be in a fishbowl; your subordinates will be constantly watching you trying to determine whether or not you are capable of handling this position. As a new Supervisor, you must know that they will be pushing the envelope in an attempt to determine how you will handle each and every situation. You have to ask yourself, do you want to put yourself through this treatment? Remember, you know this will happen because you did the same thing as an Officer to your new Supervisor. So put yourself into that situation and prepare accordingly.

Along with this position comes major responsibility and accountability (I believe this can be viewed both as a negative and a positive). No longer can you blame the Supervisor for not handling the situation properly, because that Supervisor will be you. I am not saying this is a bad thing, but you have to decide if you are willing to add this responsibility, the extra pressure, and stress, and incorporate it into your current lifestyle -- a lifestyle which may already consist of a marriage, children, mortgages, car payments, and other debts. These are tough questions and you have to be honest with yourself as you determine if you are willing to make the necessary sacrifices and accept the position.

Your life, in general, will change. What do I mean by this? Well, you will be viewed as "different." You are no longer one of the "boys." You must now set the example for others to follow. Your social encounters will change because you will now be the person who may have to discipline the same person you used to have dinner with prior to your promotion. Now you may say this will never happen but trust me, it does. It may not happen right away but as soon as you make your first decision that does not set well with your troops, it will happen. The minute you correct your "friend" or take disciplinary action against him, it will happen. The minute you take corrective action against one of your friend's friends, it will happen and when it does, you will not believe it at first. But then you will realize that you *are* different and that you no longer have the same relationship with those people who used to be your friends. When you accept this responsibility, you will have made the transition from Police Officer to Supervisor.

Having said all that and how it will affect you, you must now explain this phenomenon to your spouse or significant other. Like you, they will also say that these prior relationships are too strong and your position would never influence their friendship. But believe me, it will.

Try this on for size: My partner and I worked Homicide for six years. During this time, we were as thick as thieves while on duty. Then he introduced me to his sister-in-law. Soon we became brothers-in-law as well as partners in the Detective Bureau. So far, no harm no foul. Then I got a promotion and all of a sudden I was his Sergeant as well as his Homicide partner *and* brother-in-law. This was all well and good until the first disciplinary action against him from yours truly. It doesn't matter what the discipline was. Even if only a verbal reprimand, it has an affect on the relationship, both on duty and off. You can imagine how it would affect family functions, etc. Enough said. It is something to discuss with your loved ones, and hopefully, it will never happen to you.

Too many Supervisors have stated to me, about three months after being promoted, "I never expected anything like this, and my wife doesn't understand why I have to spend so much time at the station. When I was a street cop, I was able to come right home after my shift. Our friends don't call or come over as often as before, which bothers my wife a lot." It is not all dark and gloomy, but I would be remiss if I did not give an honest look at both sides.

Chapter 4

Honest Reflection

Now that you have finished reading the above sections, sit in a quiet area with a notepad and draw a line down the center of the page. On the left side, write down what you believe are the positive reasons for becoming a Supervisor with your Department. On the right side, write down the areas of concern you believe might occur if you were to become a Supervisor.

Now that you have made an *honest* and *objective* list of the PROS and CONS of promoting within your agency, take this information and discuss the entire situation with your spouse, significant other, or anyone else that may be affected by your promotion. You must be upfront and extremely honest because when you are promoted, your life will change considerably.

Chapter 5
Let's Talk About Preparation

The purpose of preparation is to raise the bar so others must participate at your level!

First and foremost, don't be shy about your intentions. Let your Supervisors know that you are planning to promote and that you are willing to handle all assignments, especially those with responsibility. Make your intentions known and take advantage of your promotional opportunity by approaching the process with a positive, upbeat attitude! I remember an Officer who at every possible opportunity told me that he was going to be my next Sergeant. He also saw my wife at a car wash and told her the same thing, and you know what?—He was!!!

The promotional process should be one of the best experiences of your career. You are about to embark on an outstanding journey that will change your life forever.

Many people have asked me over the years what they need to do to prepare for their promotions. My response has always been: education-education-education. Bachelor Degrees are as common as an A.A. Degree. More Officers are obtaining their Masters Degree, so it is incumbent for you to remain competitive in the promotional process, and the more education you have the more competitive you will remain.

Will you automatically get the position because you have completed your education? No, but it will demonstrate to the raters and your Chief that you have initiative, and you strive to constantly improve yourself. Besides, it helps to move that gray matter around in your brain.

Now I know that going to school will take a lot of time away from your family and areas of interest but you must realize (and again I ask that you remain positive in this endeavor) that in order to remain competitive, and obtain the position that you desire, sacrifices must be made.

As Chief, I did not appreciate excuses from my personnel for not continuing their education, and there were a number of them. For example: Officers would say they didn't have enough time off to enjoy themselves so they didn't want to take what time they did have and go to school. Other statements consisted of: "I just had a child and I want to spend time with him"; " the cost of schooling is too high, and the Department doesn't reimburse my tuition"; "shift work makes it impossible"; "my spouse doesn't see me as it is, and if I go to school it will cause problems at home"; "education is not that important- if they don't know who I am and what my abilities are by now, then education is not going to help me obtain my goal."

I am not a complete Ogre and I realize that there are certain times when returning to school are tough, especially when you are assigned undercover details or other specialty assignments that have irregular hours. **BUT** going to school doesn't mean that you have to attend everyday and take a full course load. If you can take one class a semester or every other semester, you are still demonstrating initiative in achieving your goals.

While being a husband with a beautiful and supporting wife, and a father with two very young children, and while working in Patrol, and then in Detectives it took me ten years to complete two years of college to obtain my Bachelor of Science in Police Science. So I know and understand the difficulties but I kept working to complete this phase of my education, and it eventually paid off.

If you want to make excuses, and you think that education is a waste of time, then it doesn't appear that your future career (or the upcoming promotion) is very important to you. So if you want to show initiative and go for that promotion, find a solution that will work in your situation and move forward in attaining your goal.

Along with education, there are other areas you can research to help prepare yourself for the Assessment Center and/or your Oral Board presentation. Take time to expand your horizons and read as much as possible on various subjects. There are many good books depicting the leadership roles in Law Enforcement. Read two or three, as they are good reviews, but also go outside the box and read other books on leadership that have been written for the private sector. For example, Tony Robbins, Tom Peters, Warren Bennis, Lee Iacocca, and former New York Mayor, Rudolph W. Giuliani have written excellent books on leadership and management. I would also recommend books written by coaches and military personnel, such as basketball coach and player Pat Riley, the biography of Green Bay Packers football coach Vince Lombardi, or Army Generals such as Colin Powell and "Stormin" Norman Schwarzkoph – All are people who had very different personalities and styles and you either loved them or hated them but above all, you respected them. They were not afraid to take risks, and they motivated their personnel; they learned by their mistakes, and they thought outside the box. Status quo was not good enough for them. They were innovators who were always looking for ways to improve themselves and others.

The **International Association of Chiefs of Police** has produced a brochure entitled "Police Leadership Development Reading List," which provides a number of leadership books that are worth investigating. You can obtain this brochure by contacting the,

- **U.S. Department of Community Oriented Policing Services, U.S. Department of Justice,** or by writing to:

    International Association of Chiefs of Police, 515 N. Washington Street, Alexandria Va. 22314 USA.

Leadership is leadership. It doesn't matter whether you are in Law Enforcement or the private sector, you are dealing with people who either work for you or who are your customers. Yes, your citizens are your customers and your job is to provide leadership for your personnel, which in turn will help to provide the best possible customer service.

Besides reading books, there are other ways for you to improve, such as listening to various self-improvement tapes. There are time management and motivational tapes on cassettes or CDs. There are numerous authors, like Ken Blanchard's *One Minute Manager*; Stephen Covey's *7 Habits of Highly Effective People*; Wess Roberts, Ph.D. *Leadership Secrets of Attila the Hun* and the world's greatest salesman Zig Zigler, to name a few.

Don't feel you have to follow everything these authors say, because you don't. Some ideas may not be your style, but they will give you something to think about. There may be a few areas that you don't like about yourself and should change. Self-evaluation is a good tool and should be an ongoing process. I can guarantee you that the person I was as Chief of Police was not the same person who started out as a rookie cop 37 years prior. We mature, create different career goals, and visualize a different future for ourselves, personally and professionally. This ongoing self-evaluation process is really great because if you don't change, you will become stagnant, which, in turn, will cause boredom -- and eventually you will burn out.

How Do I Prepare for the Position?

Technically, you have been preparing for this position since you were first sworn in as Police Officer. Remember how each year your Supervisor gave an annual evaluation or performance report and the results of that evaluation were, hopefully, discussed with you? If they were not discussed, set up a meeting with your Supervisor and have them explain what process they used to evaluate you and if you have questions or disagree with their evaluation, now is the time to discuss it with them. Normally, you are told of your strengths and weaknesses and areas in which you can improve. Your evaluation *should* be used as a training tool and with that in mind I know that you have taken the advice from your Supervisors and developed your career accordingly. That is why you're now ready to proceed in moving up the ranks of your Department.

We have discussed preparing for this promotional process by education, research, reading, and discussing evaluations with your Supervisors. So what can you possibly do next to improve yourself? Since we have just started, you must realize that this is only the tip of the iceberg, you have a lot to accomplish before you are ready for your promotional exam. There are two areas of concern that I feel are extremely important, and necessary for achieving a successful conclusion to this process. One is getting physically fit; the other is becoming mentally tough.

Physically Fit

Prior to participating in any physical activity, <u>consult your Physician</u>.
I'm sure as a Police Officer you try to keep yourself in decent physical shape, but now it's time to make sure that you are receiving proper nutrition as well as continuing your weight training and aerobic training. A properly balanced diet will help you think on your feet while under stress, especially during this testing process. There are numerous books on this subject. Two that I particularly

enjoyed are *Keep the Connection* by Bob Greene and *Dr. Bob Arnot's Guide to Turning Back the Clock* by Robert Arnot. M.D. These books will describe how weight and aerobic training, for example, will help you get into better shape and feel good about yourself.

The reason I push getting in shape is: If you *look* good, your clothes fit properly, you *feel* good and an air of confidence develops, which can give you an edge during this competition and as you know every little bit helps.

So, think about your diet and exercise program, and remember to get a proper night's sleep. These three essentials will not only make you feel better but will assist you in gaining the confidence and stamina you will need throughout the testing process.

Remember: When you walk through that door, you only have **one chance to make a first impression** and believe me, the raters will take into consideration the way you look and carry yourself. You must demonstrate that you care about yourself, while looking professional at all times. Think about it: If you feel good, look good, and have a great command presence when entering the room for your Oral Board or Assessment Center exercise, *you* start off *in control* of the situation.

Mentally Tough

What do I mean by becoming mentally tough? You'll find during this promotional process that it is a very draining experience, both emotionally and physically.

Therefore, what I am suggesting is that you make yourself as tough as possible to face this experience so that you will be able to handle any situation that may arise. One of the first things about becoming mentally fit reverts back to the prior section of becoming physically fit because, basically, it all has to do with how you feel about yourself -- the way you look at yourself in the mirror each morning. I believe, if you are physically fit and feel very good about yourself, then you are stronger mentally.

For example, when I was preparing for advancement, I would place myself in the position of the rank I was attempting to achieve. Let's say I was trying for a Sergeant's position (this would also apply to a Detective, Senior Office, Lieutenant, or Captain's position... well you get the picture). The first thing I had to do mentally was develop a mindset that I was in fact a Sergeant. I would start by placing a set of Sergeant stripes on my bathroom mirror, so that those stripes would be the first thing I would see in the morning while getting ready for work. This would give me a mental edge; it was helping me feel like I was a Sergeant. Remember, this is not a situation where you wake up one day and say, "Today I wish to be a Supervisor," and a wand is waved over your head and *presto* you *are* one. No, this is a position that you should have been preparing for since the start of your career. So don't take it lightly. What we are attempting to do now is develop a mental attitude that will give you the advantage over your competition. So, you put the Sergeant stripes on the mirror and each morning as you prepare for work you constantly look at those stripes as positive reinforcement and you start thinking like a Sergeant.

Part of being mentally tough is knowing who you currently are and who you want to be. What you have been doing for several years, whether you realized it or not, is grading how well your Supervisors fulfill their responsibilities. In other words, how do your Supervisors actually supervise? Remember when you were a rookie Police Officer? You would always observe the best Officer on your watch and try to emulate their actions. You would observe the way they approached a scene, handled a field contact, and how they interrogated or interviewed suspects and witnesses. Then you would try to utilize those techniques and eventually developed your own style. On the other side of the coin, you would also observe Officers of lesser quality and analyze their approaches and procedures to insure that your style of enforcement did not parallel theirs. The same is true in developing yourself as a Supervisor. Throughout your career you've been watching your Supervisors and how they operate out in the field and with other personnel. You made assumptions regarding these Supervisors: likes and dislikes regarding their techniques; how they treat their subordinates; how they respond to emergency situations; how they present an aura of calm when everyone else is falling apart; command presence, and how they are professional with high integrity; they just bode confidence in whatever they do. This is the type of Supervisor you enjoy working for and want to emulate.

Of course, there are the other Supervisors that don't quite meet your expectations, and you also have to analyze their actions – and you all know the kind I mean: This is the Supervisor that does not demonstrate command presence and you wonder what the Chief was thinking about when he appointed him or her!

In both of these circumstances, you take the good and the bad of what you observe, place them in your Supervisor "bag of tricks," and develop your own Supervisory style – one in which you emphasize the strong points of leadership and supervision and negate the poor qualities that you don't wish to develop in your style. Now you are becoming your own person with your own style of leadership. You are developing someone with whom **you are now comfortable.**

Now, with the proper mindset, you watch how Supervisors that you currently work for handle various situations. Afterwards, get some quiet time and think about how you would have handled the situation if you were in charge. Debrief the entire scenario. Determine the positives and the negatives, and be honest while doing so. If your Supervisor handled the incident properly, then give him credit and learn by it. If you felt there were areas for improvement, **DO NOT** contact this Supervisor and give him your opinion, because it is not your place, probably would not be received in a very positive fashion, and it is certainly not necessary--just learn by it. Try to analyze various situations throughout your tour of duty. Give yourself quizzes by asking yourself: How would you explain the situation to the Lieutenant? Did you properly handle various situations with the resources available to you at the time; how would you handle a disgruntled employee; would you recommend discipline (if so, how much)? With this mental attitude, you begin to feel like a Sergeant. Suddenly your attitude changes and you are looking at various things in a different light, which will give you an advantage over your competition because you are now developing the feeling of a Supervisor rather than that of a Police Officer. And this mindset has to feel good, you have to feel comfortable with it, and it has to become your clothing. In other words, **you have to own it!**

Now that you feel better about yourself because you are becoming physically fit and developing a strong positive mental attitude, you will become more confident with the process. With your stripes posted on your bathroom mirror in the morning and your observations of your Supervisors' actions in mind, you begin to think, "I can do this job just as well as they can, if not better, so what's the big deal?"

Well, we've only just begun to crack that nut. In many ways, you are far ahead of your competition, but you still have a long way to go. Again, this is just the initial phase to get yourself into a mindset as to why you want this promotion and the best way to achieve it.

The reason I mention not becoming too sure of yourself is because of a personal situation that occurred many years ago when I was first testing for a Sergeant position. At the time, people were telling me that I was ready to be the next Sergeant, and there was no doubt that I would make it. I thanked them and continued to prepare for the written exam. I was reviewing the Sergeant Test questions from the Davis Company Handbook and was feeling pretty good about the process. But I kept hearing over and over again that I was the heir apparent for the

Sergeant's position, so pretty soon I started to believe it. I just knew that I was going to be the next Sergeant, so I let up on my preparation because I had it in the bag! (You can see where I'm going with this, right?) I took my first ever Sergeant written exam and was pretty sure that I passed and would be the new Sergeant. But when the results were published I found out that I had failed the written with a score of 69% (and I needed 70% to pass)! Wow, what a blow! What was really strange was that all of those people who were hawking my virtues suddenly were absent from my world. I was standing alone and totally embarrassed because I thought -- *no I knew* --I had this position "in the bag."

After a couple of days of feeling sorry for myself, I reexamined the process I utilized for obtaining this position and determined that I did it entirely wrong. I listened to everyone else rather than myself. I stopped trying so hard because I knew the position was mine. I didn't make the sacrifices necessary for the position. I felt that because I was Elvin G. Miali, they would hand me those stripes without hesitation. From listening to everyone around me, I felt I was bigger than the game itself and there was no way I could fail. (Well if you ever want to fail miserably, then follow this pattern and you can join me in being one big un-promoted jerk!)

Throughout this book I will mention that you must always look for the positive in every negative situation, which is exactly what I did. Although I didn't realize it at the time, my inability to pass the written examination was a blessing in disguise and really changed the direction of my Law Enforcement career. After whipping myself for a couple of days, I made a new goal that I would always place number ONE in every future promotional examination, which would require much more efficient study habits and far   better research on every case or issue that would be representative of recent trends.

For example, today, I would learn more about the American with Disabilities Act (ADA) or the Police Officers' Bill of Rights, or whatever else is in vogue at the time of the exam.

In the situation just described, I interviewed everyone that could assist me in achieving my goals and attempted to prepare myself for every situation that could possibly occur during the testing process – all of which helped me to become mentally tough and rather than being afraid of upcoming competition, I looked forward to it. I had prepared to the best of my ability and was ready to demonstrate why I should be chosen for the position. This was a pretty lofty goal, but it worked for me. It doesn't mean that they always selected me for the position but at least I made their decision very difficult.

Some candidates have a very difficult time expressing themselves during an interview. They can take written exams and pass them with flying colors, but they freeze up on a face - to - face interview outside their normal Law Enforcement activity.   How can you overcome this problem? Well, actually it is not really a major obstacle and can be corrected quite easily. There are professional organizations such as Toastmasters International that assist individuals who are nervous about speaking in public. There are also speech classes at various colleges that assist you in writing and presenting speeches to audiences large and small. There are many reference books on this subject, such as *"Never be Nervous Again"* by Dorothy Sarnoff, which covers techniques for the control of nervousness in communicating situations.

Finally, the approach that really helped me prepare for public speaking and make various presentations was a drama class I took at a junior college. This may sound very funny to you -- or you may ask how can that assist me with public speaking? -- but I can assure you, it really helps. First of all, it develops your self-confidence because you have to act in front of groups of your peers and oftentimes, you may make a fool of yourself. This is not always a bad thing because you learn to laugh at yourself, which is extremely necessary in order to be successful in life. Additionally, it helps you to learn to project your voice when you are speaking, especially in a small auditorium without the benefit of a microphone.

These activities help you to overcome your fear of being in front of an audience. Basically, we are always acting, one way or another, because the way we act on the job is not necessarily the way we act when we are off duty. We speak differently when we make contacts at work. We don't talk to our wife, kids, friends, and relatives the same way we would a field contact (at least I hope you don't). So, these classes help a potentially shy person (like me) or a person that is nervous in front of audiences, overcome their concerns. My drama class was a lot of fun and helped me become a more confident speaker, especially when it came to Oral Board and Assessment Center exercise presentations. (As a side note, the class also assisted me in my fieldwork and improved my interview and interrogation techniques. I eventually overcame my stage fright and was even chosen to play the part of Saint Joseph in the college Christmas play. Now *that* was a great experience!)

Chapter 6

Completing the Application

OK, now that you have your new tough mental attitude in tune, you must prepare for your written examination. After completing your formal application, you may be requested to complete a supplemental application that recaps your Law Enforcement career. The application may include information on your experience and the various positions you have held, either with your current Agency or former Law Enforcement agencies. It may also include information on commendations, discipline within the past two years, sick leave usage, college education, certificates achieved, a review of your evaluations for the last two years, and anything else that the Administration may feel is important in order to make an intelligent decision regarding the position.

At the end of this supplemental application, the Department's Chief of Police or his designee may add some additional questions not associated with the formal written examination.

For example, I would ask questions similar to the following:

To Sergeants, I would ask:

- Describe your problem solving experience; or

- Identify three tasks within the Uniform Patrol Division of the Police Department that you would consider as priorities if you were assigned as a Sergeant in that Division. Explain why you chose the particular tasks, your plan for accomplishing them, and how the Department would benefit from your actions.

To Lieutenants, some questions might include:

- Describe your experience involving the motivation of subordinates to perform to the best of their ability. What methods do you think are important to facilitate productivity?

- What methods do you use to keep informed of what is going on in your area of supervision? What controls do you have? What do you do when procedures don't work well?

To Captains, I might ask:

- Explain how you have utilized your leadership philosophy in motivating and disciplining. How has this style of leadership improved the effectiveness of our Department?

- There appears to be a decline in individuals who want to become a Police Chief.

  o Why is that?

  o What would encourage you to consider that position?

o If you are not interested in becoming a Chief, why not?

To Sergeants, Lieutenants, and Captains, I would ask the following:

- Personal Attributes: Describe your perceptions of your competence in each of the following areas:

  A) Interpersonal skills

  B) Analytical Skills

  C) Administrative Skills

  D) Leadership

  E) Self-Control

Submit the information in rank order by listing the attributes you perceive as your strongest area first (#1), followed by your next strongest second (#2), and continue through your least strongest (#5) as your fifth response.

These are just a few of the questions I have used. Other questions may include how you would respond to hypothetical situations; ask for information regarding recent court decisions; or your Department's General Orders, Administrative Orders, and Special Orders. (Your Agency may call these orders or procedures by different names; just make sure you are aware of them and know where to locate them within the Department).

These extended applications may be utilized in various ways, such as by the <u>Oral Board</u> or by members of the

<u>Assessment Center</u> in an effort to develop a better understanding of each candidate.

Many Agencies incorporate a Supervisor's round table panel that will review the candidates' applications and addendums and then independently rate them prior to the Oral Board examination. Some administrators will *only* use this information to assist them in making their final decision, while other Department Heads may use a rating system, which encompasses the Supervisors' round table discussion, the candidate's application, extended application, resume, and the last two evaluations. After each Supervisor independently records their score, they submit it to the Personnel Manager who will give it a percentage -- anywhere from 30-50 percent -- towards the candidate's final score.

As you can see, the application and extended application process are very important. Sometimes it affects up to half of your total score; therefore, do *not* take any shortcuts when filling out the forms and compiling the information. Be as accurate as possible. Don't guess! Your Personnel Department has your personnel file and you have every right to review it, so do it. Remember, if you've had discipline in the past two years, or whatever timeframe the application states, be sure to include it. Now is the time to change a negative situation into a positive one and if the discipline situation is brought up during your Oral Board or during any interview connected with the testing process, take advantage of this opportunity. I truly feel you have been given a great opportunity because you now have a chance to explain the situation and how you have learned from the error of your ways. Also, you will be able to explain how the discipline has made you a much better officer because you are now able to assist others so they don't make the same mistakes you did.

These applications and resumes are read by the panel and, therefore, it is important that you make them as neat and professional looking as possible. If your typing skills are poor and you do not have someone that is capable of adequately typing your application, take it to a professional typist and for a small fee, you will have a product that you will not only be proud of but one that will also demonstrate your professionalism and your seriousness about making a positive statement during this promotional process. Now, having said that, make sure that the typist does not go overboard with your application presentation. Remember: The idea is to **keep it professional.**

Prior to submitting the application package, be sure to contact your Personnel Manager and ask them if there are any criteria relating to the presentation of the application. For example, some agencies do not want it bound with spirals, staples, or other types of attachments.

The reason I bring this up is because in the past, some Officers have presented their application packages with shoulder patches attached or have written their documents on pastel colored paper. One Officer even wrote his application by hand, which does not present a very professional document and made me question whether the Officer was taking this process seriously. **Remember, keep it professional!**

Chapter 7

Preparing for the Written Examination

After you submit your completed application package, you are ready to begin to prepare for the written examination. There are a number of promotional manuals on the market. Arco, Payton, and Davis publishing companies have manuals for Sergeant and Lieutenant promotional exams. I am not advocating any particular one. Check the Internet, or go to "The Legal Book Store" or check at your local bookstore if you wish to obtain one.

You'll find that the questions in these manuals are normally written in a different format than what you may have been accustomed to while taking your college exams; therefore, you should become familiar with this style.

The written examination is the most important phase of the testing process, because if you fail this exam, there is no tomorrow. So, I urge you to study hard and prepare yourself accordingly. If you feel you are ready for this exam, review some more, and continue to do so until the day before the exam. Take as many practice tests as possible so you become familiar with these types of exams and the way they are written. This will help eliminate any surprises on the day of the exam.

If at all possible, include your family when you begin to study. For example, your spouse, significant other, a child, or a friend can read you the questions from the manual and you can give them the answers while sitting outside watering the front lawn or while sitting together in the backyard. This is a nice way to bring them into the promotional process. Remember, they are under just as much stress as you, so try to keep them involved as much as possible. Your family should understand why promoting is very important to you, and how they will be affected when you are promoted. Your goal is to get them on board so that your goal is equally important to those you live with.

There will be other times, while doing research on such things as case law or reviewing the regulations and General Orders of your Department, where you will need a quiet area such as a library or your home-office, if you have one. If you explain this to your spouse or significant other ahead of time, I'm sure they will understand that the sacrifices you are making today will be very beneficial to the family in the future, after you obtain your promotion.

The night before the exam, relax. Have dinner with your family. Eat a light meal, and do not drink any alcoholic beverages because doing so may inhibit your sleep. And go to bed early! If you live near the ocean, take a walk along the beach and, again, relax. Do not try to cram for the exam because this will only confuse you. If you don't know the material by now, another 15, 20, 60 -- minutes or even an "all nighter" -- is not going to help. So go to bed knowing that you have done all that you could do and be confident that you will do your best tomorrow.

"If a man does his best, what else is there?" —
General George S. Patton

On the morning of the exam, get up early, take a shower, get dressed, eat a good breakfast, and leave with plenty of time to spare so that when you arrive at the testing location, you will be relaxed and not rushed or harried. You will feel a little knot in your stomach; don't panic because the knot is a good thing, as it helps to keep you on your toes and give a better performance.

There are a wide variety of exams that are used for the written examination process. Some exams will test your knowledge, while others may test your abilities. Some come directly from the state, while others may be designed by your Personnel Department. Many tests are based on a few basic types of questions, which may include:

1) Writing an Essay

2) Sentence completion

3) Verbal analogy

4) Number series

5) Configuration series

6) Hypothetical situations

When the day of the written exam arrives:

- Sit away from a window and do not sit next to a friend as these may prove to be distractive.

- Do not take stimulants, such as "no doze" or excessive caffeine as they may cause a loss of alertness or a mental "crash."

- Read the directions of the exam completely. It is very important that you follow these directions because failure to do so may cause you to be disqualified or fail the exam; various studies have demonstrated that oftentimes a poor test-taker has a tendency to misread the directions and jump to conclusions.

- Know ahead of time if points are deducted for unanswered questions. If they are considered wrong answers, be sure to answer all of them even if you have to guess.

- Be aware of your time schedule; don't stay on one question for a long period of time. If you are not sure of an answer, move on and if you have time at the end of your exam, return to the question and any others that may have caused you a problem.

- Always work the easy questions first, and then return to the difficult questions; this is also true for the essay questions.

- Remain confident and positive; just because you don't know one or two answers is not the end of the world. These exams are developed to push your knowledge. You are not expected to obtain 100%!

- If you complete your exam early, don't rush out of the facility. Instead, use this time to review your questionable answers.

- DO NOT READ INTO THE QUESTIONS. Answer the question the way it is written. All too often we analyze way too much and soon lose the intent of the original question.

- Know how to properly answer the exam questions. Do you circle the answer or the letter, or do you fill in the blank?

- Pay attention to important terms when reading the question, such as most, not, best, opposite, may, or shall.

Use sound reasoning techniques. Think through the questions but, again, don't over analyze!

Good luck! You're on the right track.

Chapter 8

Preparing for the Oral Interview

This process is now becoming very exciting because even though you passed your written examination, your placement on the eligibility list will depend on how well you perform during the Oral Board or Assessment Center Exercise.

A guide entitled, *How to Prepare for and Pass Promotional Exams,* published by the California Peace Officers' Association, stated the following regarding the interview process: "The reasons for the interview should be obvious. The Department would like to have as its representatives, men and women, whose leadership, common sense and self assurance will reflect credit upon the Department."

On many occasions, I have observed that candidates who passed their written examination with high scores met their "Waterloo" during their Oral Board presentations. Many candidates have demonstrated poor judgement in tactical situations, unusual mannerisms, immaturity, lack of leadership abilities, or anger and quick tempers. The stress is enormous and oftentimes, the unprepared candidates will fall apart and demonstrate that they are not as good as their written scores depicted.

When preparing for your Oral Interview or Assessment Center Exercise, you will have to do some research. You must determine what qualities your Chief of Police is looking for in his Supervisors. The best way to determine this is to contact the Chief and request a meeting to discuss the upcoming promotional exam. Now, before you say I couldn't possibly do that because the Chief is too busy or I don't think he has an open-door policy, remember that the Chief is looking for a Supervisor that can be depended upon and one that demonstrates initiative in handling difficult situations. What's the worst thing that can happen? The Chief will tell you that he will not discuss the process with you and if this occurs, you are no worse off than before. In fact, you may be in a better position because you have demonstrated to the Chief that you are interested in the position and displayed your initiative in this process.

Also speak with the City Manager to determine what he is looking for in a Supervisor. This will help you to obtain a feel for what the administration of the City and your Department Head is looking for in their management personnel.

As a Police Chief, I always felt it was beneficial for the candidates to know exactly what my expectations were, and then they could decide if they wanted to be part of my team. I had an open-door policy that allowed the candidates to come and discuss their concerns with me, but it was up to them to take the initiative to speak with me first. Naturally, I could not tell them what questions the Oral Board would ask because I didn't know. However, what I could do was to advise them, as I am doing with you now, on how to prepare for the oral examination and give some insights into how they could improve their performance during the testing process.

Some Chiefs may not adhere to this type of counseling, but it was my style for 17 years and was comfortable for me. My personal feelings are that the best way to get your people to understand the type of Supervisor you're looking for is to tell them face-to-face and if they have any questions, you can clear the air at that time. If you discover that your Chief will not discuss the process with you, go to the next highest command level Supervisor and request a meeting. Find someone who has been through the process, knows the Chief's philosophy, and is willing to talk with you. Once you find them, be a sponge, soak up every bit of information possible, and ask all of the questions you feel are relevant to the testing process. Discuss areas regarding what the Chief is looking for as it pertains to leadership traits and management styles.

Another question you may ask is how much independence does the Chief allow his Supervisors out in the field? Does he want his Supervisors to micro manage subordinates, or does he give his Supervisors free rein? Ask everything possible so that you feel comfortable and can be happy working as a Supervisor in this environment. You don't want any surprises because if you are not happy in this position, it will affect everything you do in Law Enforcement as well as your personal life.

Determine what _your_ leadership style is. There is no leadership style that is best. There are a number of books that discuss the various styles utilized by today's leaders, Including: autocratic, situational, and participatory with the latter being laissez-faire. It may be difficult for you to define exactly which style fits you, so take the time to determine how you would operate out in the field handling various situations as well as your personnel. When you are comfortable with this style, name it, then be ready to explain to the raters how this leadership style fits you.

For example, I always considered myself a "situational leader," which basically meant that I would act according to the situation at hand. There were times that I would ask others to give input or participate prior to making my decision. Other times, I would immediately take control and make the decision without any outside assistance which would be described as autocratic. I don't recall ever utilizing a laissez-faire or laid-back style of leadership.

This is a very short synopsis of leadership styles and how I use them, but make sure you have your own style and don't just *copy* mine or anyone else's, because it will only get you in trouble when you try to be somebody you're not. You must be comfortable with the style you have chosen; if you're not, the raters will see through your façade. Also, if you use a leadership style that "is not you," your subordinates will question your motives and become confused. This confusion or uncertainty as to what you want and who you are could cause dissention in the ranks, which in turn will demonstrate your poor leadership qualities.

Know the difference between leaders and managers, if there is one. I always liked the statement made by Ross Perot, ***"People cannot be managed – inventories can be managed but people can be led."*** Determine how you feel about this. I personally feel that the terms "leaders" and "managers" are the same because you can't have one without the other. Whatever your feelings are regarding this argument, be prepared to defend it if the Board challenges you.

"The elusive half step between middle management and leadership is grace under pressure."— JFK

Remember that defining your leadership style is a necessary part of your research, and it will assist you immensely during your Oral Board or Assessment Center Exercise presentations. While gaining this information, you will find yourself developing more and more confidence in your ability to compete, which in turn will assist you in gaining an edge on your competition. Remember, gaining an edge on your competition is the purpose of being well prepared.

OK, you have spoken with the Chief, his Command Staff, and anyone else you respect and feel can assist you. But your work is just beginning. It doesn't matter whether you are involved with an Oral Board or an Assessment Center Exercise; the preparation is always the same.

In your research, you need to become *familiar* with your Department's General Orders as well as your Administrative Rules and Regulations. Talk to your Department's legal adviser, your City Attorney, or your Police Officers Association's legal representative. Try to contact someone who is knowledgeable with current case law, especially in matters of Skelly, The Police Officers Bill of Rights, discipline, the American Disability Act, and Megan's Law, to name but a few. Also, be confident in your knowledge of your Department's policy on Use of Force and Vehicle Pursuits and any other **"hot ticket items"** that may be alive in your Department or community. Know them forward and backward, inside and out. Read the newspapers to determine what is happening in other communities and around the country regarding Law Enforcement activities, and determine how these activities may affect you and your Department.

Speak with someone in Finance, and discuss how the budget is prepared. Know the amount of the City's budget and what percentage goes towards the Police Department. Know the type of budget your City uses. Is it a *line item* budget, a *program* budget, a combination of the two, or some other type of budget not mentioned? Does it have a 5 or 10 year forecast? Again, ask questions until you are comfortable with the budget process. Now, you may not think it is necessary to know about the Department's budget, but it is. It is true that other personnel may be handling the budget process for the Department, but as a Supervisor you will be responsible for certain items or programs in the Department's budget. You may not receive any questions concerning the budget during the testing process, but wouldn't it be nice to have the answers in the event that one of the raters wanted to determine just how much preparation you really did during this process?

"Describe the type of budget you are working with?" was always a question I would ask, both as a rater and as Chief, when I was having my interview with a candidate. It didn't matter if the candidate was trying for Senior Officer (two stripes), Sergeant, Lieutenant, or a Captain's position; I expected them to have some idea of the Department's budget. How would you know if you were going over budget if you didn't know what the budget was to begin with?

If your Department has a **Mission Statement**, be familiar with its contents. Does your Department participate in Community Oriented Policing? If so, know what it stands for and determine how you feel it benefits or doesn't benefit the community and the Department. Be prepared to defend your answer. Also, if you believe it can be improved upon, have a plan in mind so you can explain it to the raters in case they want to hear your opinion. I always believed in a quote by Henry Ford: "Don't bring me your problems, bring me your solutions." Part of your plan should include how you will get your troops to buy into this philosophy. Remember, it is a *philosophy* not a program. Again, this is something to think about.

Chapter 9

What Do I Wear?

Dress for success, but don't go overboard and become too trendy.

Men, there is power in a good tailored suit, a freshly pressed shirt, and a new tie. Also remember that the shoes you wear should match your suit and definitely should be highly polished. The heels should be in good condition and not worn down. Don't wear Patent- leather, uniform dress shoes. They have a special need with your uniform - not with your suit. Leave your gold chains, bracelets, and diamond pinky rings at home. I would also advise against any lapel pins during your presentations. As a reminder, be sure your haircut, facial hair and sideburns are within the Department regulations, unless you are in a specialty assignment and your Supervisor gives you permission to maintain your hair out of regulation. Also, do not wear earrings during your interview. If you're not sure about accessories for your ensemble, seek assistance on the Internet or contact your local men's store that will be more than happy to discuss your options.

Ladies, the saying "dress for success" applies here and, thankfully, you have many styles from which to choose. According to Ilse Metchek, Executive Director of the California Fashion Association, "Women need to think about how they portray themselves. You don't want the attention to be on your clothing, you want it to be on your work." Keep things simple. Keep make-up to a minimum and in good taste, and utilize soft colors for your fingernails. Again, if you are not sure about accessories and make-up, you can check on the Internet or consult your local women's store for assistance.

For both the male and female candidate, be sure your fingernails are properly trimmed and clean. Make sure your hygiene is impeccable. Remember, the last thing you want to show are underarm stains on your suit, shirt, or blouse. You also do not want to emit an embarrassing odor of any kind.

When wearing cologne, aftershave lotion, hand lotion, or perfume make sure the scents blend nicely. Apply your perfume or aftershave lotion a couple of hours prior to your appointment so it has a chance to dissipate.

Men, get a haircut a couple of days prior to the Oral Board. If you dye your hair, make sure the roots are evenly colored.

Ladies, if at all possible, have your hair cut and or styled prior to the Oral Board; and if you color dye your hair, be sure your roots are not showing.

Many of these items sound so basic you may ask yourself why I am even bringing them to your attention. Well, the truth of the matter is that each of these situations has occurred with several candidates when they appeared before me as a rater on an Oral Board or during the Chief's Oral, and it wasn't a pleasant experience. Candidates have appeared with exceptionally bad body odor or heavy dandruff, which created a very poor impression. Other areas that will detract from your presentation are wearing shoes that have scuff marks, worn heels, or shoes that look as though they were polished with a candy bar. Take the time to look, and feel good about yourself, and the dividends will pay off in the future.

YOU ONLY HAVE ONE CHANCE TO MAKE THAT FIRST IMPRESSION!

Chapter 10

MOCK ORAL BOARDS

"Tell me and I'll forget; show me and I may remember; involve me and I will understand."— Chinese Proverb

You may have given speeches, handed out citations, talked to your family and friends about your career, but I doubt if you have ever sat down and studied yourself after your presentations or how you reacted in a stressful situation. Now people may have approached you and stated you did well but ask yourself: Is "well" good enough to beat out my competition?

What I strongly suggest is that you **videotape** yourself while answering questions during a mock Oral Board. I don't want you to ask yourself questions while sitting in front of a mirror to watch your reactions because you will miss many of them. And I don't want you to stand by yourself and ask yourself questions while standing in front of the camera. Nor do I want your significant other or a close friend to ask you questions while you are sitting in front of a camera. Why not, you may ask? Because you want to feel the stresses associated with the testing process, especially the Oral Board or the Assessment Center Exercise, and the above situations do not initiate enough "real life" pressure. So, there's no stress in messing up in front of your friends or significant other; they are very close to you and may have difficultly giving an honest critique of your performance. It is difficult to tell a close friend that they "stink." Plus, since they are friends, it is too easy to laugh it off if you make a mistake.

No, I want you to contact three respected associates, from an outside Agency, and ask them to be raters on your mock Oral Board. If possible, the rank of the raters should be at least one rank higher than the position for which you are testing. Since these individuals are well-respected Officers whom you admire because of their achievements within their agencies and throughout their careers, you would probably feel embarrassed or upset with yourself if you performed poorly in front of them. Ask them to put you through the "ringer." They will take this assignment seriously and will work diligently on being an excellent Board and will rate you accordingly.

Now that you have your Oral Board ready, pick a date, time, and location away from your residence. Your home is way too comfortable and doesn't place enough stress on you. Remember, we are attempting to recreate the intensity of your upcoming testing process. You may have access to an office on a weekend when no one is around. Try to utilize a conference room with a large table. Usually, during an Oral Board presentation, the room is arranged with three seats for the raters on one side of the table and one seat for the candidate on the other side. Place your video camera behind the raters' chairs so it is facing you. If you don't have a camera, borrow or rent one for a day -- it is well worth the rental fee. Have one of the raters turn the camera on prior to you entering the room. This will help evaluate your entrance: Did you demonstrate self-confidence, command presence, or were your shoulders slouched? Do not have anyone "man" the camera as this will create a distraction for you.

Prior to entering the room

As previously discussed, when you were preparing for the written exam, the night before the Oral Board, I want you to relax as much as possible. If you live by the water or a park, take a walk with your significant other and understand that you have prepared yourself as best as possible and that you are ready for tomorrow's process. Have a light dinner with no alcoholic beverages, and go to bed early.

Set a time for your presentation: arrive early, dressed the way you would during your "real" presentation. In other words, if you are planning to wear a suit and tie or a dress to your "real" Oral Board, this is what you will wear to your mock Oral Board.

Remember, this is just like a dress rehearsal for a play only in this scenario, you are working extremely hard to enhance your future, which is what makes this preparation so exciting. The reason I compare it to a play is because once you enter that room, you will be on stage, and all eyes will be on you while you give an outstanding performance, convincing these raters that you are the best candidate for the position. This preparation also allows you to plan your presentation ahead of time because during an Oral Board, there will be a time limit. It usually depends on your City Personnel Manager and sometimes the Chief of Police, but normally the Oral Board will last anywhere from 20, 30, 45, or even 60 minutes. This is the time that you have *to sell yourself* to the panel of raters, so you must be ready.

Prior to arriving at the location, do some facial exercises. As you know, the mouth is a muscle that must be exercised to work properly. When you wake up in the morning, you just don't jump out of bed, ready for the day. It takes a few minutes for you to stretch and rub you arms and turn your neck a few times, and then you are ready to stand up. Well, your mouth also needs to be stretched and rubbed so it will work properly when you are ready to speak. Professional singers and speakers do exercises prior to a performance, and so should you. While driving in your car, begin to stretch you jaw and lips. Start to say A, E, I, O, U in an exaggerated way so that you stretch the muscles of your mouth. Also, utilize the saying, "How now brown cow," which will help to loosen the muscles in your mouth and awaken your vocal cords. People may look at you in a funny way while you're driving, but just smile, keep up your exercises, and let them wonder what it is that you're doing.

Since we are performing this mock oral as if it were the **real thing** there are several things to consider prior to entering the room:

Remember that knot in your stomach we discussed earlier, prior to the written exam? Well, the knot helps to place you in a more competitive environment. What I mean by this is that it makes you ready for the process to begin. It gives you an edge and makes you sharp. The knot I'm discussing is a slight tightness in your stomach, not a pain that has you on the ground moaning or causes dizziness or fainting spells. You don't want to place that much pressure on yourself, because if you were in that much pain you would probably be in the emergency room prior to the beginning of your testing process. I always had a knot in my stomach prior to any testing process, speeches, or presentations that I made. I found that the knot in my stomach helped me give the best performance that I had in me. I also realized, as you will, that once the process began, the knot would disappear because I felt prepared and in control of the situation.

Something else to consider is that you are very nervous and your gastric juices are flowing and your breath may become somewhat harsh, so I would suggest that you carry a breath mint and use it just prior to your interview. Be sure it has completely dissolved before entering the room or remove it from your mouth. It is the same for gum -- don't chew it during the interview. I suggest you don't chew it at all on "game day" because you may forget about it and walk into the room and begin chewing without even realizing it. You will look like a cow grazing in a field and the moment you realize that you forgot to remove it from your mouth, you will lose your concentration and your presentation will suffer.

Entering the Room

When you enter the room, stand tall with **command presence**. There is nothing worse than watching a candidate timidly enter the room, looking scared stiff. Maybe you are shaking on the inside but demonstrate confidence on the outside. Show the raters that you are in control and confident. I remember there was a deodorant commercial that stated "never let them see you sweat," so don't.

Let the raters introduce themselves and repeat their names as you firmly shake their hands while maintaining eye contact. Now, take your seat, pull the chair up to the table, and then place your hands either in a flat position or fingers interlaced or the palm of one hand on the top of the other hand, on top of the table.

Pulling the chair closer to the table is not an aggressive move but merely a move that demonstrates your confidence. There was one Assessment Center that I participated in as a candidate, and the raters placed the candidate's chair approximately six feet from the table. Many of the candidates entered the room, sat in the chair without moving it, and held their interview over six feet from the raters. These raters placed the chair away from the table to determine which candidates had confidence in themselves to move the chair closer to the table and begin their interview.

Do *not* place your elbows on the table nor form a steeple with your fingers in front of your chin. Try as hard as possible to keep the palms of your hands flat on the table. If you place your hands on your lap, this could cause your shoulders to stoop (and you may not even be aware it is happening) or could display poor posture, which again shows body language that can be interpreted as a lack of self-confidence or low self-esteem. Placing your hands on the table helps promote correct posture throughout your interview. Then, too, if you are like me, and have some Italian blood coursing through your veins, it will be next to impossible for you not to talk with your hands, but try to keep the gestures at a minimum, and be aware of what you are doing with your hands.

While sitting, do not lean back in your chair or cross your legs, as this gives a poor impression to the raters. It makes you look too relaxed and can depict an air of aloofness, or it may be interpreted as "low self-esteem" because you are trying to look too "cool" and imply this testing process is "no big thing." Lean forward with your chest close to the edge of the table and both feet flat on the floor. This will help you remain in a position that will further your command presence at the table.

Opening Statements

Prepare an opening and closing statement. Usually, the Board will begin the session by trying to have you relax. They will say something to the effect, "Why don't you tell us a little bit about yourself." This is your time to shine. Tell them what they want to hear. State how many years you have in Law Enforcement; explain your various assignments; highlight those assignments that had command responsibility (i.e. S.W.A.T. team leader, Personnel and Training Officer for the Department, K-9 Officer responsible for coordinating an area search of a crime scene, etc). Then, explain your education achievements and your current education endeavors. Remember to just highlight these accomplishments because you are on a time schedule. Practice this ahead of time so you are comfortable with it. Make it yours but do not memorize it because the minute you stumble, you may have difficulty getting back on course. You are already nervous -- don't make it any harder on yourself. **Be concise.** You will be surprised how much information you can deliver in a short period of time if you plan your statements ahead of time.

Let the Process Begin

When the questions begin, listen to the entire question before answering. Don't think you know the answer and interrupt the questioner prior to him finishing the question because you may guess incorrectly and you will also appear rude. Chances are you will only have to wait a few seconds before the rater finishes his question and then you can proceed to give your answer. When you answer the question, be sure to look at each rater. Look them in the eyes when you talk to them. Do not let your eyes wander or dart around the room; this gives the impression that you are unsure of yourself or do not know the answer. Start with the person who asked the question, and then rotate to each of the other raters. Do this in a flowing motion so as not to look robotic. When you speak, be sure to project your voice so the raters will not have to strain to hear you; but on the other hand, don't shout. Your mouth may be dry; if they offer you water, utilize it. It is placed there for your use, and it won't be marked against you. If you can draw on other answers you have given when answering the current question, it will look as though you can pull together different kinds of information and organize it in a meaningful manner.

When you first begin to talk, your voice may quiver due to nerves. Don't let this bother you, just overcome it. Clear your throat, take a deep breath, and continue speaking. Don't tell the panel that you are nervous; they understand this because they have been in your position several times. When you begin to answer their questions, keep your hands away from your mouth so as not to block your answers. Also make sure you don't do anything to distract the panel, such as tugging at your ear, pulling strands of your hair and winding them around your fingers or cleaning your fingernails while you are answering their questions.

Remember, you are not writing a report, so don't answer in the form of a report. When you are asked a question, respond in a clear smooth cadence such as you would experience in a regular conversation. Don't chop it up with "cop slang" or sound like you're testifying in court. For example, if you are given a hypothetical situation where you are in charge, and a disturbance occurred, don't use the following terminology to answer the question: "After receiving a call of a P.C. 415, I responded to the location in question and immediately made contact with the victim and necessary witnesses. I put out an APB and then deployed my personnel to circulate through the neighborhood in an attempt to locate the "perp" and other individuals who may have witnessed the incident, etc."

As you can see, this type of answer does not flow and makes you sound very stiff. Tell the raters exactly what you would do at the scene. Explain that upon arrival you would evaluate the situation, effectively utilize your available manpower to contact witnesses, maintain a perimeter to contain the area and attempt to locate and arrest the suspect or whatever else you felt would be necessary to complete the scenario. My point here is to keep your answer to the point and avoid unnecessary articulation and cop slang.

What if I Don't Know the Answer?

Tell the truth! The raters do not expect you to have an answer for every question; they are attempting to determine your breadth of knowledge. If you try to fake the answer, the raters will know and **will** mark you down accordingly on your final score.

One time when I was taking an Oral Board exam, the rating panel asked me for the definition of "MBO"? I gave them a blank stare and, in my mind, I immediately thought that I had "blown" this competition because I had no idea what those initials meant. I looked at each rater and told them, "gentlemen, I don't have a clue what MBO stands for; but I can assure you that when I leave this room today, I will look it up for my own edification." What I eventually found out was that MBO stands for "Management by Objectives," which was a new "buzz" term utilized by Tom Peters in his *Search for Excellence* book. Thankfully, I was chosen for the position and when I spoke with the raters after the process was completed, to determine how I could improve myself for the next promotional opportunity, they basically told me certain areas of my presentation that could be tweaked -- but what really hit home was their assessment of my MBO answer. Each rater told me they were impressed with my honesty in explaining my lack of knowledge in this area. They mentioned that many of the candidates tried to "bluff" their way around the answer, which really hurt them in the final ratings. So, basically what I'm saying is that if you don't know the answer to the question, tell the raters the truth and explain that you will find the answer as soon as the process is over. Hopefully, there will only be one question where you will have to explain yourself in this manner; but whatever happens, do *not* let this incident throw you off-balance. Maintain your focus on the next question that the panel will be asking. Remember, you can't "un-ring" a bell -- what happened has happened, so let it go and move on to the next question. It's not the end of the world, and you still have time to impress the raters with your other answers. Remain positive--look what happened to me!

How Do I Answer the Questions?

The best way you know how. Give the answer you believe is correct. If the answer needs an explanation, give it but keep it concise; remember, you are on a time schedule, and the raters may cut you off. **So don't ramble!** Practice being concise; give a lot of information in a short period of time. This way you won't become flustered during your presentation. Remember to *talk* to the raters in your own style; don't sound like you're writing a police report. Police reports are very "matter-of-fact," and they only report the facts relating to the incident. If you are given a hypothetical situation, think about your answer and tell the raters exactly what you would do to successfully handle the incident or whatever it may be. The raters may try to "push" you on your answer to see if you really believe in what you're answering. If you feel confident that you are correct, don't be swayed to change your opinion. When you answer these questions, put some feeling in your answers: show the Board that you are emotional, have genuine feelings, and have a passion for this position.

When you answer questions, don't use words with which you are not familiar. Many candidates I've interviewed seemed to get their words from the *Readers' Digest* *"W*ord of the Month Club" and didn't have a clue how to use them properly or know what they even meant. They were trying to impress the panel of raters but in the long run, they really hurt their chances of scoring well. You don't have to be an English major but on the other hand, you don't want to sound like a dolt, either (just thought I would throw that in to see if you were paying attention).

The key when answering a question is to find a common ground. You don't want your answer to be too long because you will start to ramble (and, remember the time limit!). If you use too much time answering one question, your interview may be cut short and you will not have enough time to answer all of the other questions. On the other hand you don't want your answer to be so short that you don't get your point across.

There are no ground rules for answering questions. You have to say what feels natural to you. However, there is one area that created several problems for me when I was a rater. (And remember this is only my opinion; I don't really know how other raters feel about these types of answers).

Oftentimes a panel of raters will ask a question similar to this:

"If we don't choose you for this position, which candidate should we choose?"

Think about what you would say in a situation like this. How would you answer the panel? If you put down your competitors, you'll sound conceited. How are you going to feel about yourself when you tell the Board that your friends competing against you are not as good as you? Or, on the other hand, maybe they are as good as you and to be a good friend you should tell the board how really great your friend is and they should get the position if you were not chosen. This is an interesting quandary.

There was once a Lieutenant, along with other members of the same Department testing for a Chief's position. Naturally, this was an open test and Officers from other agencies were also testing. Now this Lieutenant wanted the new Chief to come from within his Department so when he was asked the question, "If we don't choose you for the position, which candidate should we choose?" he immediately stated something to the affect: "Gentlemen, if you don't select me for this position, then the only person to hold the Chief of Police position for this Department is Captain So & So!" Now, he did not stop there; he continued to extol this person's virtues and how it would be a great mistake for the Board to go outside the Department and not pick this Captain. He was quite pleased with himself when he left the room and even

72

boasted to other officers how he told the Board whom to choose. To answer your obvious question, neither he nor the other individual was selected. Rather, the Board chose a Captain from an outside agency.

If you were to give an answer similar to the above, that you feel someone else is really qualified for this position, it would appear to me that you have very little confidence in yourself or your abilities. It also demonstrates that you feel the other candidates are better than you and they should get the position, which often occurs.

On the other side of the coin, when you are asked the above question, do not "put down your opponent" because these types of answers can backfire. It will not make you look any better in the eyes of the raters but will, in fact, make you look very insecure with yourself.

For example, some Officers will answer this question by stating something like: "Officer Joe should not even be considered for this position because I have more time in grade and more education. He doesn't believe in school and only registered for classes when he heard that this promotion was going to take place. He doesn't even believe in all of your policies like I do, and he can't be trusted. Look at my record and when compared to his, there is no comparison. I am the better person." Or, "I don't think you could possibly be considering Officer Jane because she has no self-esteem and would make a terrible Supervisor. Besides you don't want a female Supervisor running your troops out in the field. You need me."

Naturally the above statements are somewhat exaggerated but believe me, I have heard similar statements during Oral Board presentations as well as in the Chief's interview. These types of answers tend to show that the Officer does not possess a great deal of self-esteem and in my book, this is definitely not the #1 candidate for the position.

So, what do you say when a rater does ask you these types of questions? Well, the first thing you want to remember is that your competition is just that - your competition; they are not your friends during this testing period. They are trying for the same position as you; they are attempting to enhance their career the same as you; they want to improve their salary just like you; so, as you can see, they should not be viewed as your friends during this testing process, but instead as your competitors.

You may feel that this kind of thinking is cruel. You couldn't possibly think that way about individuals who are your friends. These are people you depend on for assistance out in the field; whom you socialize with when you are off duty. How could you possibly think of your **friends** as **competitors**? Because, to repeat, this is a competition and should be viewed as *strictly business*!

When I was asked: "If we don't choose you for this position which candidate should we choose?" during a promotional exam, I always felt there was no other competition and I would state something to the effect: "If I were not chosen for this position, I believe the Board would be making a mistake by not giving my Police Department the best person for the job." Then I would explain why I felt I was the best person for the position. Again, you have to feel comfortable with this kind of response (for example, I always thought that if I wasn't the best person for the job then why go through all of this trouble to begin with?)!" With this type of answer, I did not give the other candidates any "accolades" (let them earn them on their own) nor did I "put anyone down." I wanted the Board to focus their attention only on me and my achievements.

"Nothing demeans you more than your demeaning of a fellow competitor!" Anonymous

Now, specifically for female candidates, there are some answers to certain questions that do more harm than good during your presentation before the Oral Board or the Chief's interview. For example, some female Officers have stated to me, "I will be your first female Supervisor if I am appointed" or "It would be good public relations for the Department to show that you are an equal opportunity Chief by promoting me" or "I hope you don't think that because I am a woman that I cannot do the job." Don't demean yourself by placing these conditions in your answers. The raters and the Chief know you are qualified to take this exam; otherwise, you would not be in the testing process. Just how qualified you are for the Supervisory position will depend on your prior work history and the answers you give to the Oral Board and during the Chief's interview. So, state who you are and why you think you are qualified for this position **based on your own merits.**

Closing Statements

In an Oral Board setting, when the raters have completed their questions, they will usually say something like, "This is your time, is there anything else you wish to add?" It is at this point that you would give your *concise* closing statement. Usually, this statement will be a recap of what you had just said. For example: "As you can see I have worked extremely hard throughout my entire career for this position. Given the opportunity, I am confident that through my various assignments, especially those in command positions, as well as my continuing education, that I have gained a breadth of knowledge that will assist the Department in the development of its personnel. Also, I will not only continue to improve upon the service the Department gives the citizens of our community in providing a safe environment for everyone, but will also improve upon the high standards for which we are known." You can include whatever fits your needs but as you can see, this is a very short recap of your entire career history and goes directly to the point that you are the person that should be chosen for the position.

When you have concluded your closing statement and the Oral Board thanks you, and they begin to stand, you should also stand and again look each of the raters in the eye, shake their hand, and thank them by using their rank and name. For example: "Thank you, Lieutenant Swan," then turn and walk out the door with your head pointed forward and your eyes looking towards the horizon. Maintain this posture all the way out the door because you are being observed by the Board until the door closes. The reason I bring this to your attention is because I have observed many individuals slouch their shoulders and hang their head while walking out the door because they felt they did poorly during their presentation. Don't let the raters know how you feel as this may -- and I repeat *may* -- have some influence on their final appraisal of your entire interview. Besides, you really can't determine how well or poorly you did because you were under so much stress that you probably don't recall every action or question that took place during those last 30 or 45 minutes of your life. How many times have you heard people say when they left an exam, "Boy, I really blew that test!" when in reality they passed it with flying colors; or on the other hand, "Boy, I aced that one!" and later found out they failed. So don't jump to conclusions (and remember what I told you about my experience with "MBO"!).

Feedback

Now that you have completed your mock oral, take a deep breath and sit down with the raters and ask them to critique your performance. You may get some hard hits, but try not to take it personally. Remember, this is a learning tool, and you want the raters to be honest with you and help you in improving your presentation. Do *not* get discouraged. This is the time to change the negatives into positives. Don't say, "Well, that is the way I am and if they don't like it, then too bad because I am not going to change." Uh-uh, wrong attitude because in reality it may be the time to change. Remember, we are not the same person that we were when we were first sworn in as Police Officers. We evolve with time and mature. We must change or grow stagnant.

Be open to any criticism from the raters -- that's what this whole process is about – and let them assess you while you take notes. When they have completed their critique, ask questions on how you can improve. For example, if they say there were parts of an answer they did not understand, discuss it with them and figure out a way to improve that answer. If they stated you rambled, determine how you can be more concise with your answers. And if they did not like your appearance or your gestures, make sure you have the answers on ways to improve any concerns prior to the rater's departure. This is your future we are discussing and these raters have taken a lot of time to assist you, so take the time to pick their brains and utilize their experience.

When the raters have left, take the time to sit down alone and review your mock oral tape. See if you agree with the raters' critique and again determine ways you feel you can improve your performance. You will notice things that you can't remember doing (i.e., facial tics, gestures, eyes wandering, stuttering, the use of "ah" throughout your presentation, and so forth). Again, take notes and be tough on yourself.

On the other side of the coin, compliment yourself for a good presentation. Build on the strengths of your actions and answers. This process gives you visions of improvement and strengths, so always be positive and utilize these areas to your advantage.

When you have finished your solo review, ask your significant other, partner, close friend, or relative to review the tape with you. These people know you the best and may be able to assist you in determining if the person they see on tape is the "real deal" or someone they have never seen before. They may determine that you look and sound great or very phony. They do not have to have any experience in your profession; they are rating you on your appearance and how you present yourself to a group, which is very valuable feedback.

What Do I Do With This Information?

Initially, nothing! You have just been through a very stressful situation, so I want you to take a couple of days off and relax. Get away from it -- go to the show or out to dinner -- but forget about it. After two days have passed and your brain is starting to function again, it is time for you to get back to work in developing the best candidate for the position.

Review your tape again and remember, as Tony Robbins always states, "Repetition is the mother of learning." After reviewing your tape, compare the tape with your notes. You may observe other areas for improvement or see more strengths that you originally missed. When you are finished with the tape, make a complete list of areas for improvement, and then list your strengths. When you have completed these lists, it is time to build on them. Any areas that you need to improve will take precedence. If you gave an incorrect answer, research the correct answer and write it down. Don't leave it to memory because you will forget it and this way you will have a resource to refer to when you continue your studies. If your gestures were excessive, you now know that you must control them. This will come with practice now that you are aware of what it is that you are doing that detracts from your presentation. Build on your strengths, which will give you confidence for your next Oral Board. If you handled some very hard or complex questions well, remember that feeling and utilize it in the future. If you looked great in your new clothes, be sure to duplicate that look and stand tall because when you look good on the outside you feel good on the inside.

Again, this is part of your research and development and after correcting any deficiencies you may have noticed or had pointed out to you during your presentation, you may feel that you would like to have another mock Oral Board, which would help you determine if you have eliminated the troubled areas of your former performance. (I highly recommend this idea.) Utilize another team of raters for the Board and follow the above steps throughout the process. This will help build up your self-confidence and helps eliminate some of the mystique when you are making your presentation before the Oral Board. Remember, more preparation makes you a more viable candidate.

Chapter 11

Assessment Centers

Assessment Centers are not new. In 1991, the California Police Officers Association distributed a booklet entitled *The Art and Craft of Assessment Centers,* which stated Assessment Centers were used by the German High Command in World War I to select officers with exceptional command or military abilities. During World War II, Assessment Centers were used by the Office of Strategic Services (OSS), a forerunner to the CIA, to select spies. Many private corporations utilized the Assessment Center format for promoting management personnel long before it was tried by public safety organizations.

In the late 1970s and early 1980s, Law Enforcement began to use Assessment Centers in selecting management personnel. During this time, Paul Whisenand, Ph.D., and George Tielsch, Ph.D., were two of many advocates of the assessment approach and wrote a book called *The Assessment Center Approach of the Selection of Police Personnel,* which explains in detail the Assessment Center approach and all of the dimensions it evaluates.

I will not go into much detail here except to state that these Assessment Centers are designed to measure certain attributes or qualities of the candidate. These attributes or qualities are referred to as "dimensions." The following dimensions, as listed in the CPOA book, may change with each Assessment Center and how it is organized; therefore the following common dimensions should be utilized as guidelines only:

Oral Communications - Ability to orally communicate accurately and clearly information, ideas, tasks, directives, conditions, and needs to groups or individuals, with or without time for preparation.

Written Communication - Ability to communicate in writing using proper grammar and syntax in an organized, accurate, and concise manner.

Problem Analysis - Ability to identify problems, secure relevant information from both oral and written sources, identify possible causes of problems, and analyze and interpret data in complex situations involving conflicting demands, needs, or priorities.

Judgement - Ability to evaluate courses of actions, develop alternative courses of action, and reach logical decisions based on the information at hand.

Organizational Sensitivity - Ability to perceive the impact of a decision on the rest of the organization, awareness of the impact of outside pressures on the organization, and awareness of changing societal conditions.

Planning and Organization - Ability to efficiently establish an appropriate course of action for self and/or others, to accomplish a specific goal, and make proper assignments of personnel and appropriate use of resources.

There may be other dimensions used along with the above, again depending on how the Assessment Center is developed and by whom. These other dimensions may include:

Initiative - Desire to actively influence events rather than passively accepting them, self-starting, and takes action beyond what is necessarily called for.

Interpersonal Relations - Ability to perceive and react to the needs of others, paying attention to others' feelings ,and ideas, accepting what others have to say, and perceiving the impact of self on others.

Independence - Ability to act based on your own convictions rather than through a desire to please others.

Development of Subordinates - Ability to maximize human potential of subordinates through training and developmental activities.

Persuasiveness - Ability to organize and present material in a convincing manner to gain agreement or acceptance.

Delegation - Ability to use subordinates effectively and to understand where a decision can best be made.

Listening Skill - Ability to extract important information in oral communications and to convey the impression that one is interested in what others have to say.

Decisiveness - Readiness to make decisions, render judgements, take action, or commit one's self to a course of action.

Leadership - It is very difficult to describe this term but it involves a number of attributes, usually measured in management Assessment Centers, and has been described as autocratic, democratic, dynamic, inspirational, and telepathic. It is viewed both as passive and active. Leadership involves the ability to communicate; to be independent; to make decisions; to plan and organize the work of one's self and others; to analyze problems; to take risks; to be self-starting, flexible, and sensitive to others.

The authors of the CPOA book state, "...any effort to measure leadership as an independent dimension will probably be inadequate and misleading." (I agree with this evaluation.)

Once inside the Assessment Center, you will be observed by a group of raters who will score your performance. Typically the candidate's score is rated on a scale between 5 (as the highest) and 1 (as the lowest). A score of 5 indicates the candidate is **Strong** in that category. A score of 4 indicates the candidate is **More Than Adequate** in that category. A score of 3 indicates that the candidate is **Adequate or Acceptable** in that category. A score of 2 indicates that the candidate is **Less Than Adequate** in that category, and a score of 1 indicates the candidate is **Weak** in that category.

Assessment Center Exercises are either group or individual and while the format of the exercises is basically the same, the content changes, depending on the job level and organization. Basically the Assessment Centers Exercises will consist of:

- A **Group Discussion** will start without an appointed leader. During the exercise, the participants with leadership ability will assume leadership of the group.
- An **In Basket** exercise simulates the working situation in which some work is generated by documents assigned and forwarded to the

candidate. Difficulty and stress can be increased or decreased by controlling the amount of time, the number of individual items, and the complexity of the items.

- A **Written Problem** requires the candidate to review a certain amount of material and prepare a written report. The report could be (but is not) limited to performance evaluations, budgeting requests, staff reports, or press releases.
- An **Interview Simulation** could simulate any number of situations in which the candidate must interview others for a job.
- An **Oral Presentation** requires the candidate to make a formal presentation to a group of persons who are usually the raters.
- A **Social Gathering** is a situation where the raters will evaluate you on your interaction with others.

Following is a brief overview of the Assessment Center. If you are going to participate in an Assessment Center, your preparation is basically the same as for an Oral Board, only your testing process may be extended anywhere from one day to a five-day evaluation. The best advice I can give you is to be yourself and don't fight to take control of a situation. A good leader assumes control while allowing his competition to make the mistakes. I don't mean that you should sit back and say nothing, but listen to your fellow competitors, quickly analyze their statements and if you agree with them, expound on what they said to make it yours. If you disagree, then do it in a respectful but strong manner, which will make people take note of your position. Be sure you are correct in your statements because you will either live by them or die by them, but don't be afraid to make the decision! Above all, remember that you are in competition with the others in the Assessment Center.

The following examples are given as areas of concern so that your actions, or lack thereof, will not be misinterpreted. You are being continually evaluated as you go through the process, so always keep your guard up.

Case in point:
When I was competing for the Chief's position at Fountain Valley, I was going through the Assessment Center Exercise, which was being conducted by a renowned consultant in the Assessment Center field. I had completed many of the exercises along with my fellow competitors, and we were standing around during a break having coffee. I spoke with a few of the candidates but I also wanted some alone time to concentrate on my performance. Later, during the interview process of the Assessment Center, it was brought to my attention that I had been observed during the breaks as not intermingling with my fellow candidates and that I was "aloof." I asked the rater to explain how he came by this conclusion, especially since I did not see him constantly watching me during the breaks. He explained that he did not always see my actions during the breaks because he had other matters to attend to but when he did observe me, I had little interaction with the others in the group. Since this was affecting my rating and my professional goals for achieving the Chief's position, I had to explain my actions to him. Afterwards, he stated that he understood and that he had misinterpreted my actions. Had I not had the

ability to discuss this matter with this rater, it could have jeopardized my chances for that position.

Also, during this same Assessment Center Exercise, prior to the beginning of a session, I was sitting next to a Captain from another agency when the lead consultant "leaped" (literally!) into the room and upon seeing this Captain came rushing over to him and, in front of other candidates (me included), proceeded to expound on his impressive resume and how happy he was that this Captain was testing for the position. At first, I thought it was part of the stress program associated with the Assessment Center; but as this consultant went on and on about this candidate's achievements, I realized it was just bad judgement on the part of the consultant. These actions made me realize that I must be more conscious of the performance of others during the Assessment Center (especially, when I was involved in group discussions or other interactive dimensions with this candidate).

These are just a couple of examples with which I was personally involved. Of note is that on the positive side, they did assist me in being better prepared for future Assessment Centers.

Later, the raters may ask you to explain some of your actions during these various exercises. Don't become excessively nervous. If you have a reason for your actions, which I assume you do, give it because these exercises are designed to display who you are and allow the raters to view the way you accomplish your assigned tasks. Oftentimes your explanation could be outstanding and the raters may question it only because it was not the way they would have completed the task, and they know that there is always more than one way to complete a task.

Chapter 12

The Chief's Interview

Now that you have successfully completed the written exam, the Oral Board, or the Assessment Center process, it is usually time to face the Chief of your organization. (Some agencies may not have a Chief's interview and will pick an individual according to how they placed (1-2-3) on the eligibility list.

I always gave a Chief's interview because I had other questions regarding the Department that the raters would not ask since they were from outside Agencies and not completely familiar with the Department's inner-workings. This interview also helped me to have a one-on-one conversation with the candidate and gain more insight into who exactly this person was.

If you meet the Chief, this will probably be the most stressful interview of your entire competition. You have been selected from all of the other candidates to discuss your career with the boss.

First of all, feel good about yourself. There are only a few candidates that make it to this step of the promotional process, so remain positive and pat yourself on the back for a job well done.

You really looked good for your Oral Board or Assessment Center presentation; you want to look even better for the Chief's interview. Haircut, suit, skirt, shirts, blouses pressed and cleaned; nails trimmed and cleaned; shoes should be polished to a high gloss finish.

If you decide to wear your uniform for this interview, be sure it is in very good shape with no loose threads or buttons missing. Speaking of buttons, make sure they are buttoned. I always was very surprised when an Officer would enter my office and one of their shirt buttons would be unbuttoned. The uniform should be freshly dry cleaned and pressed. Make sure your badge is polished, more than normal, and all of your accessories or medals are properly attached. You should wear a Class A uniform without a hat, and your tie should be clean and fresh. I never did like a clip-on tie for these interviews because the metal clip was always exposed and it detracted from the uniform. If possible, have a matching pen and pencil set in your shirt pocket. Your leather gear should be clean and in good condition along with your duty weapon. As I mentioned before, polish your shoes to a high gloss, or wear uniform dress shoes if possible. If you wear uniform shoes that do not have the ability to shine, then make sure they have a fresh coat of polish or are very clean. Check yourself out in a mirror and add anything else you feel needs to be completed so that you will feel confident and make a strong statement when you enter the Chief's office.

Second, you are probably asking yourself, "What is the Chief looking for?" Good question! The Chief is looking for persons who will make the perfect match in the organization. He is looking for candidates who will have the ability to lead the organization into the future; who are developing and/or possessing many of the dimensions listed above in the Assessment Center section; who possess high integrity, loyalty, professionalism and are not afraid of hard work; who will talk with the administration if they are against a policy, but after they are heard and the decision still stands, will carry out that policy with no disrespect to the administration; who because of their abilities, will gain the respect of their subordinates and treat them in a fair manner and with respect (you don't have to be their friends but you are required to be there for them); who will be a leader, mentor, cheerleader, confidant, disciplinarian ,and can be counted on by peers, superiors, and subordinates; who has good interpersonal skills; and who can make decisions on their own and is willing to take responsibility for their actions. Most of all, the Chief is looking for someone who will represent him in the best manner, when they interact with the public or the other officers.

These are the basic traits that are being requested by your administrators. There are sure to be others and you can determine what they are when you ask *your* Chief what he expects of his future leaders.

Lastly, the Chief's interview will consist of a list of questions to determine who you are and if you meet the needs of the Department and believe in the philosophy of the administration. The Chief may want to elaborate on some of the questions asked by the Oral Board or the Assessment Center. More than likely, he will have more questions on the Department policy, budget items, liability issues, leadership traits, more hypothetical questions, and sometimes just some plain talk about family, hobbies, stress reducers that you utilize, such as working out at the gym, walking, hiking, or yoga, so he can get to know you better.

Prior to entering the Chief's office, remember to complete your facial exercises so your facial muscles are relaxed and you are ready to answer all of his questions.

When you enter the Chief's office, shake his hand firmly and take the appointed seat. Sit upright; do not slouch or cross your legs. If your jacket is buttoned, unbutton it when you sit because it does not look impressive to have a suit jacket stretching its limits when you are sitting. Answer the questions just the way you did during the Oral Board. Don't ramble; depending on the number of candidates the Chief is going to interview, you are probably on a time limit. Look directly at the Chief. Don't let your eyes wander and, again if you do not know the answer, say so, with the understanding that you will find out the answer as soon as you leave the interview.

Remember that knot in your stomach? Well, it will probably feel like a giant rock prior to this interview but remember, you are in control. Don't let the stress overpower you. Think positive. Your actions and answers got you to this point, build on that concept. You are good and you have prepared yourself for this position, so run with that thought and soon that rock will return to the little knot you want in your stomach to keep you sharp when you make your outstanding presentation.

Usually, this interview will provide you with time for an opening and/or closing statement, so take advantage of this time and give a concise statement of your achievements and how you can benefit the Department and the community when you are chosen for the position.

When you have finished your interview with the Chief, stand tall and extend your hand, even if you did not feel you did as well as you wanted during the interview. While looking the Chief in the eye, thank him for his time and leave.

Good Job!!!

Chapter 13

WHAT HAPPENS WHEN I MAKE IT

This should be one of the happiest days of your career. Celebrate with your family and friends and thank them for their support. Be sure to avoid gloating. There is a clear line between gloating and celebrating. Now, get ready for fun and a greater responsibility in developing your personnel and your Department. Remember, attitude is everything! Keep a positive outlook no matter how bad things may seem. Anyone can complain, but it takes a really strong person to rise above the din of complaints and maintain an upbeat, positive attitude. You are now a Department role model for your Officers. You are also their mentor, cheerleader and confidant. You are special because out of all the candidates that interviewed for this position, you made it! How special is that?

You are no longer their peer but having said that, you must never forget your roots. Even as a Chief of Police, I always remembered that I started as a Patrolman. This was my basis in Law Enforcement, where I was taught how to be a Police Officer. Listen to all of your personnel because, oftentimes, they have some great ideas for solving many of your problems. *Never* let the position go to your head.

You worked hard for this position so enjoy it and never be ashamed that you were chosen over someone else. There will always be someone who does not think you deserve the position, don't let them rain on your parade. I always believed that you must respect a person in order for their opinion to mean anything. People that tried to put me down or stated that I didn't deserve a position were not on my top 10 list to begin with so their opinion didn't matter to me -- nor should it matter to you.

The job is yours because you were the best candidate for the job, Congratulations!!!

Chapter 14

What Happens If I Don't Make It?

"If you continue to think the way you always thought, you will continue to get what you always got. Is that enough?"— Anonymous

You will be asking yourself, "What did I do wrong?" or "How could I have improved?" You may also feel depressed, embarrassed, humiliated, cheated, or "they just didn't want me because they knew I was not a kiss-up." These are some of the emotions and statements that I have heard or felt myself over the years.

Even if you feel this way, it is not a career-ending situation -- there will always be a tomorrow! Yes, be upset if you truly tried your hardest and prepared the best you could --and then **GET OVER IT!**

I explained earlier how I thought there was no way the Department could not choose me for the Sergeant position and I bombed it. OK, I had all of the above emotions and made the dumb statements regarding the Department, how I was the one who should have been chosen, and how I was so much better than the person they chose. Eventually, I knew I could either let it beat me down or I could **GET OVER IT** and move on with my career. This was my decision and the Department had nothing to do with it.

When you finally get over your feelings that you were shafted, or whatever they may be, learn by your experience. I have to caution you not to let this self-pity take too long. Three or four days or a week at most should suffice. You have to realize that after awhile everyone who is listening to you is tired of it and they want to move on. They will give you an ear for awhile, but don't take advantage of it.

I always advised every candidate who came to see me after the process was over that I expected them to be upset or otherwise they didn't want it bad enough. I further advised them that I paid more attention to the actions of those candidates who did not make the promotion than those that did. I wanted to determine how they dealt with adversity in the *real* world. Many candidates did extremely well and eventually attained their goals on future exams. Others went down in a ball of fire and are still to this day, grumbling about everything and continuing with the "poor me" attitude. **Get A Life!**

Analyze your performance and determine what your strong points were and where you could improve in your next exam. Be honest with yourself and determine if you studied enough or if you answered the questions to the best of your ability. Was your demeanor appropriate; did you appear unsure of yourself or too sure of yourself? Were you too nervous to remember the questions, or did you forget to answer the questions in their entirety? All of a sudden, your mind goes blank. This is often called a brain freeze, among other things. (Remember: If this does occur, it is permissible to ask the rater to repeat the question.)

Next, call the raters and ask for their input regarding your presentation. They will review your presentation in detail and explain what they considered your strong points and will usually expound on areas upon which you need to improve. Remember, they were once in your shoes and they want to see you succeed, so question them in detail but do not argue with them; they are there to help you.

If you were interviewed by the Chief or his designee, set up an appointment to discuss the results of your interview with him. This is very important because it will not only help you improve in the future but, again, it demonstrates to the Chief that you are serious about the position, and are trying to determine how to improve yourself for future promotional processes.

There is a saying, "When you lose, don't lose the lesson," and that is exactly what this experience is--a lesson to be learned. Develop it and turn the negative situation into a positive experience. You did not receive the promotion or assignment you wanted this time, but you are much better off then when you started. You know what your goals are and you are still striving to reach them; and you have a better understanding of how to achieve them the next time around. If these promotional processes were easy, it wouldn't mean as much to you when you achieve your promotion.

Continue taking exams. Many Departments have an Oral Board process for specialty assignments. If at all possible, take advantage of this and enter the process, even if you're not sure you want the assignment. Who knows, you may change your mind once you begin to investigate the position and really want a change in your duty assignment. I believe the more Oral Boards you are exposed to the more comfortable you will be when the next promotional process comes around. I don't know who said this, but it fits the occasion: "Winners make things happen; losers let things happen." Remember, you are continuing to improve upon your competitive abilities, which will put you ahead of your peers. Don't wait until there is a notice of a future promotional exam; prepare now because you never know when the next promotional process may be given.

One thing that is very important for every process in which you participate is to thank the loved ones who put up with you during these stressful times. They were with you every step of the way, and they will be supportive, no matter the results.

Chapter 15

This Is Only the Beginning

I do not have a conclusion for this book because I believe this is just the beginning for you in achieving your career goals. By reviewing the contents of "**Unless You're the Lead Dog the Scenery Never Changes**," I hope you developed a new understanding of the promotional process. I also hope that I have removed some of the uncertainty that is created when testing for these positions.

Remember that you are constantly preparing for your future. Be aggressive in this preparation and don't let others negatively influence you, especially when it comes to your career. Remain positive in your endeavors. Turn any negative situation into a positive experience. Be strong in your desires. If you fail **Get Over It** and keep trying until you reach your desired results.

Take pride in all that you do. I believe in the saying, "If there is no pride, there is no quality."

This is a great time in your career and I am excited for you because now is the time when you will make many decisions that will affect your future. It is also the time to look at your career in a different light. At first you were just trying to perfect your profession but now you have the opportunity to make changes and develop others who will follow your lead. Change is great and you are becoming a part of it. So do your best and enjoy the ride.

Good luck in all of your future endeavors in becoming the Lead Dog!

I would like to hear from you. So, if you have enjoyed this book and it assisted you; or if you have any questions or would like to have one on one counseling with me, please feel free to contact me via my e-mail: leaddogpromo@yahoo.com

"It's supposed to be hard; if it wasn't hard, everyone would be doing it!"
Tom Hanks as Coach Jimmy Dugan in the movie "A League of Their Own"

Addendum

More Good Stuff

Questions for the Chief

Oftentimes when I was speaking before a class regarding the Chief's expectations from their Supervisors, I was asked to complete a questionnaire called "Questions for the Chief." These questions are geared towards a Sergeant position, but I have utilized many of them in all ranks during the Chief's interview phase. They are to be utilized as something to think about when you are doing your research for your promotional process.

Remember, these are my answers but I firmly believe that many other Chiefs share the same view.

1. Name three qualities/traits you desire in a Sergeant?
   - Honesty/integrity.
   - Professionalism/Loyalty.
   - A sense of humor.

2. Name three things you demand in a Sergeant?
   - Set the Example.
   - Be Accountable.
   - Be Positive.

3. When you were a Sergeant, what was the one thing you would have done differently?
   - I would have taken more time to know my personnel.

4. What negatives do Sergeants do that they should not do? How do Sergeants fail probation?
   - Sergeants, on probation, run into problems when they are afraid to act or overreact. That is, they don't know how to act like a Sergeant.

5. What is the best way for a candidate to stand out from other equally qualified competition in an oral?
   - Be yourself.
   - Pat yourself on the back.
   - Don't put others down.
   - Demonstrate your knowledge and common sense.

6. What are your expectations in a Sergeant? Agency expectations?
   - To lead.
   - Monitor activities of his personnel.
   - Cheerlead.
   - Discipline.
   - CARE.

7. What is your management style?
   - Situational.

8. What obstacles do you see facing Law Enforcement currently? In the future?
   - Retention of qualified personnel.
   - Hiring of qualified personnel.

- Older community; elderly victims; run down cities.
- Hi-tech crimes – must train our officers in a different way to fight these crimes.

9. Should education be important to a Sergeant? Degrees?
   - Education is extremely important to all officers no matter what their rank.
   - AA degrees are becoming as plentiful as BA or BS degrees. A Master's degree is becoming necessary for future advancement.

10. What assignments would you like to see an Officer have in their background at time of promotion?
    - It's not so much how many assignments the Officer has had. It really depends on how well he Performed while in these assignments.

11. What personality traits do you look for in a Sergeant?
    - Positive attitude.
    - Insight into his personnel.
    - Good sixth sense.
    - Not afraid to try different approaches.

11a. What personality traits do you look to avoid in selecting a Sergeant?
    - Officers who are negative,
    - Always state, "I can't do it".
    - Complain about doing what they are paid to do.
    - Always trying to get out of work, especially near the end of their shift.

12. Do you prefer an Assessment Center or straight a Oral Board presentation for Sergeant?
- I prefer a straight Oral Board approach for all of my promotions.

13. Is dress important for the interview? Your recommendations?
- Dress is very important. It is the first impression you make on the raters.
- Keep it business attire and professional looking.
- Class A uniform is appropriate as long as it is in good condition and all of your rank, patches, and various insignias are properly sewn onto the uniform.

14. How has the role of Sergeant changed over the last 10 years, and how do you see it changing over the next 10 years?
- Today we deal with a multitude of personalities and lifestyles in the Department.
- Many Officers have little or no life experiences and still live at home.
- Administrators must explain themselves more as to why certain things are done in certain ways.
- More laws to know.
- Police Officers Bill of Rights.
- Liability issues.
- We now have a higher caliber of Officer, any Officer of rank must stay up with them or the Officers will lose respect for him or her.

15. How can I best prepare for this position?
    - Mock Orals.
    - Videotape yourself during these Mock Orals.
    - Research and study.
    - Utilize Leadership tapes.
    - Think of the Sergeant you enjoyed working with and utilize *some* of his techniques when dealing with personnel and citizens.

16. How important are opening and closing statements?
    - Very important, if they are allowed.
    - Don't memorize them verbatim, but be sure you remember all of the points you want to make; How you express these ideas will be spontaneous and fresh each time you say them. Make them "yours."
    - Demonstrates preparation.

17. COP and POP -- is there a difference?
    - Community Oriented Policing and Problem Oriented Policing are two recent buzz-words, but to me they are basically the same with the same goal.
    - They provide a service where you solve all types of problems whether civil or criminal.
    - They must be a part of the Department philosophy.
    - We were doing it long before someone gave it a name. It was called "good old-fashioned police work," of helping the community live together in a safe, quiet environment.

- If there was a problem, no matter what it was we took care of it or helped the citizen find a remedy so it wouldn't become a criminal matter.

18. Some agencies have Sergeants closer to the line Officers. Others have the Sergeant closer to management: Where do you see the Sergeants?
    - The question should be, "How does the candidates see himself or herself in the role of a Sergeant?"
    - I feel all of my Supervisors are management.
    - I would hope the Sergeant would see himself as one step below a Lieutenant rather than one step above a Patrolman. He is not "one of the guys" anymore.
    - This also applies for the ranks of Lieutenant and Captain.

19. Mission Statements… are they important? How should Sergeants implement them? Why?
    - Yes they are important; Mission Statements are the philosophy of the Department.
    - Unfortunately, many candidates do not know the basis of the Mission Statement.
    - The Sergeant is most involved with the "troops" and should know the premise of the Mission Statement so that he and his command can be on the same page when it comes to understanding the Department's goals.
    - The Sergeants must discuss the Statement with their personnel at roll call or Department training classes.

- It should be posted around the station so **all personnel,** both sworn and non-sworn, are aware of its contents.
- You don't have to memorize it, just know what it stands for, and how it relates to the Department and the citizens you protect.
- I asked all candidates to explain the Mission Statement, whether they were involved in a promotional process or trying for a specialty assignment.

Hopefully, this gives you some idea of what many Police Chiefs are looking for in their future Supervisors.

Career Development within the Department

I also advised my personnel of requirements that I expected for career development within my Department (for the purpose of this book, I utilized a generic form and did not mention any one particular city):

> It is the responsibility of the executive of any organization to inform its members on what is expected of employees in order to enhance their careers within that organization. Careers are enhanced in various ways, such as: special assignments, promotions, and job enrichment. Before any of these events transpire, it is necessary to meet specific criteria that are hereby established.
>
> These criteria in many cases reach beyond those specific areas in which employees are routinely

evaluated on an annual basis. They are standards and expectations by which those employees who will advance in this Department must successfully maintain during their term of employment with this agency.

- Effective Human Relations
Success in the organization will not be at the expense of fellow employees. Human relations skills must be displayed that provide evidence that there is sensitivity to the feelings and needs of co-workers and members of the public who are contacted on a routine basis. The paramount tenet here is that the organization's finest resource is the people who comprise the organization. People are to be treated fairly and with dignity and respect. A healthy organization depends on effective human relations.

- Goals and Objectives
It is important for all Department personnel to be aware and to do their part as team members to accomplish Departmental goals and objectives. The following two statements most clearly explain the overall goals of this Department:
    A) Strive to protect the right of all citizens to be free from criminal attack, to be secure in their possessions, and to live in a peaceful environment.
    B) Move as an organization to become ever more responsive, dynamic, and resourceful in serving the needs of our citizens.

Each employee is an integral team member and is important to achieving these goals and objectives. A sense of self-worth and self-confidence should be balanced with sincerity when attempting to achieve individual and organizational goals.

- Loyalty
Loyalty is a quality that in no way can be compromised. It is expected that loyalty will be displayed at all times to:
    A) Fellow workers – superiors and
       subordinates.
    B) The division or unit to which an
       employee is assigned.
    C) The Police Department as an
       organizational entity.
    D) The Chief of Police as Chief Executive
       Officer of the agency.
    F) The City, its city management and
       governing body of elected officials.

- Ability to Develop Subordinate Personnel
Since our personnel are our greatest assets, organizationally, it is mandatory that those individuals who aspire to advance in the Department exhibit the ability to develop subordinates, or in the case of non-Supervisors, those employees who may be junior within the organization. Many individuals possess extraordinary skills and interest in specific areas or at least the potential to develop these skills to a higher degree of proficiency.

These individuals must be recognized and given the opportunity to grow in those areas that will benefit the individual ultimately, as well as the Department or City. Along with the opportunity to develop the employee, the successful individual will provide support and guidance to assist the subordinate or junior employee in his/her own career enhancement.

- Flexibility and Adaptability
  The ability to be receptive to changes that are uncomfortable and adapt to those changing conditions is a quality that must be present before an employee can advance in the organization. One must be willing to listen to divergent ideas and opinions and make the most of adverse circumstances that may be thrust upon him/her as a result of the implementation of change. Flexibility and adaptability is that valuable ability to function with a minimum of disruption and take full advantage of the ideas and concepts that arise as adjustments are made to change in our environment.

- Past Performance
  Employees who are to be considered for advancement in the Department will have displayed consistent exemplary performance in their respective job assignments. Improvement of noted performance deficiencies, if any, must be consistent and lasting.

- <u>Sensitivity and Awareness of Our Work Environment</u>
  It is the absolute responsibility of each aspiring employee to acquire the knowledge necessary to appreciate the various exclusive characteristics of the City – its history, organization, political components, citizenry, and philosophy. Once this knowledge is acquired, it is expected that a degree of sensitivity be ever present in dealing with these various elements that comprise the City.

  The philosophy of the City is:
    A progressive, dynamic and caring organization moving in concert with clear direction—
    o Committed to the highest quality of service to the community;
    o Fostering a spirit of loyalty, mutual respect, and trust; and
    o Striving to attain the next horizon.

This information, in my estimation, is very important for you to know and follow no matter what position you may be testing for. It is the foundation of any Agency, and every administrator that I know is looking for men and women who adhere to this philosophy.